The How and Wow of the
HUMAN BODY

From Your Tongue to Your Toes
and All the Guts in Between

By Mindy Thomas and Guy Raz
Illustrated by Jack Teagle

Houghton Mifflin Harcourt
Boston   New York

To our Wowzers all over the world . . . this is for you. —MT & GR

To my wife, Donya, and my family,
thank you for all your amazing support. —JT

All rights reserved. For information about permission to reproduce selections from this book, write to
trade.permissions@hmhco.com or to Permissions, Houghton Mifflin Harcourt Publishing Company,
3 Park Avenue, 19th Floor, New York, New York 10016.

hmhbooks.com

The illustrations in this book were done digitally in Photoshop.
The text was set in Benton Sans.
Cover design by Mary Claire Cruz
Interior design by Mary Claire Cruz and Abby Dening

Library of Congress Cataloging-in-Publication Data is available.

ISBN: 978-0-358-30663-4 (paper over board)
ISBN: 978-0-358-51299-8 (signed edition)

Manufactured in China
SCP 10 9 8 7 6 5 4 3 2 1
4500814441

CONTENTS

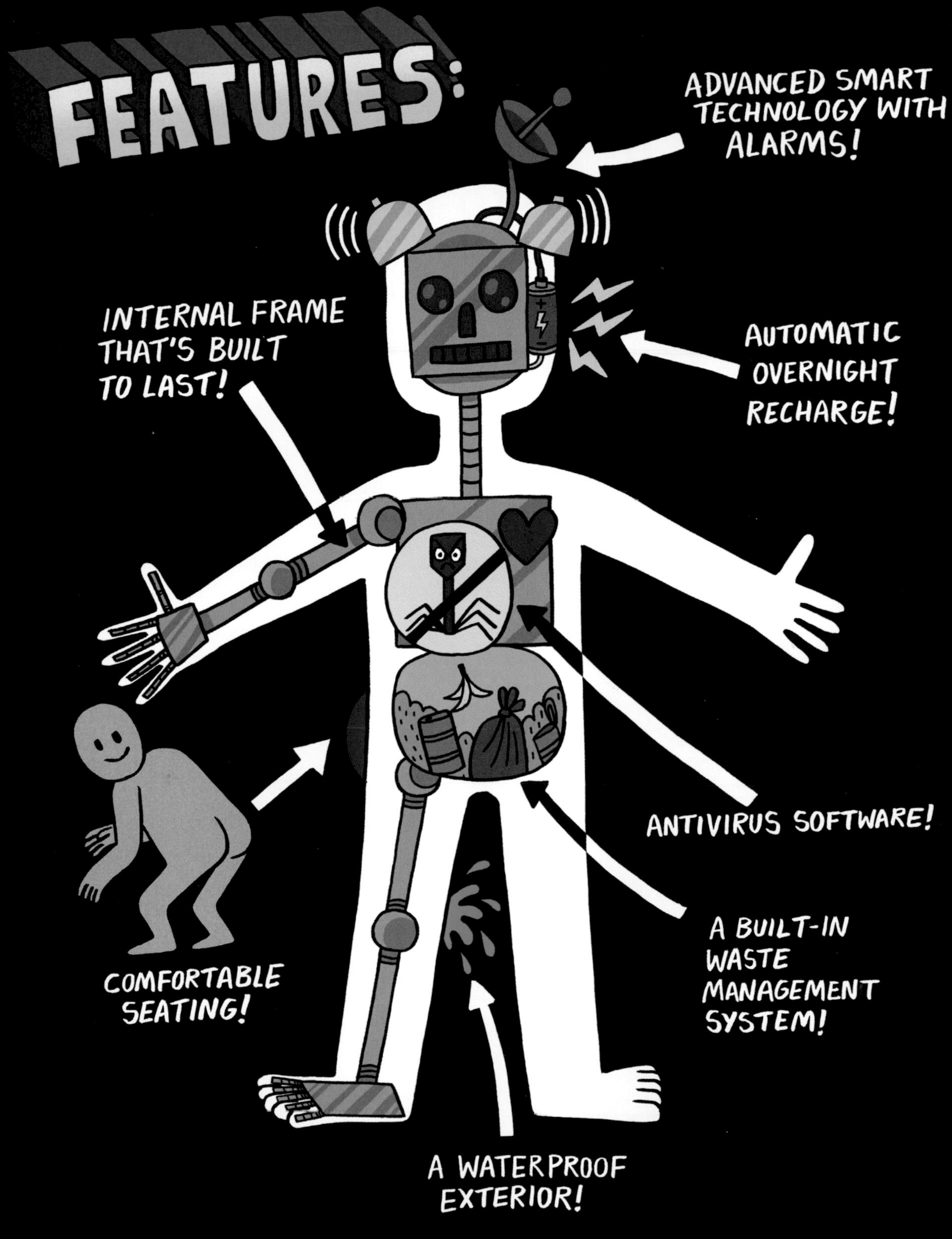
FEATURES:
ADVANCED SMART TECHNOLOGY WITH ALARMS!
INTERNAL FRAME THAT'S BUILT TO LAST!
AUTOMATIC OVERNIGHT RECHARGE!
ANTIVIRUS SOFTWARE!
COMFORTABLE SEATING!
A BUILT-IN WASTE MANAGEMENT SYSTEM!
A WATERPROOF EXTERIOR!

INTRODUCTION
WELCOME TO YOUR BODY!

Seeking some serious wow in your world? Well, look no further than your own body! For *you* are a walking, talking, barfing, breathing, pooping body of *wow!* Your body is a custom-built piece of mobile machinery with a lifetime guarantee!* (*Length of lifetimes may vary.)

In these pages, we will take you on a top-to-bottom tour of your insides and your outsides, exploring how in the world your body works for you.

Now, before we get started, here are a few dos and don'ts for experiencing this book:

Yeah!

Whoa!

DO read it out of order. Some books are meant to be read from front to back. This is not one of them. (Dip into the parts that grab your attention—unless of course *everything* interests you, in which case start on page one and keep going!)

DO spill the beans to friends and family about what you discover in these pages. You will be filled with new and interesting wows, and if you don't share them, you might explode.*
(*That is a big fat lie.)

Interesting!

DO grab a shovel and do some serious digging if you want to learn more about a particular body part. There is *lots* more to discover. If we included every bit of information about every single bit of your body, this book would weigh more than a bus! With a train on top!

DON'T hand this book to a baby. BABIES. EAT. BOOKS.

DON'T barf all over this book when you get to the gross parts. And there are *lots* of gross parts. You are gross. And so are we. And so is your grandma. Being gross is part of what makes us human.

That's dangerous!

Don't do it!

Gross!

DON'T use this book to kill a bug. Bugs have bodies too.

That's it! Enjoy! And know that we love your guts.

Mindy and Guy

THE HEAD

LET'S START AT THE TOP

Eyes
The One-Way Windows of the Face

Nose
Let's Get Nosey

Ears
Hear Ye, Hear Ye!

Mouth
The Biggest Hole in the Human Head

 **EYES**

The One-Way Windows of the Face

For sighted people, the eyes are one of the most important organs of the human body. These slimy Ping-Pong balls are largely responsible for helping you understand and interpret the world around you—using more than two million moving parts and eye muscles that move more than a hundred thousand times a day! And thanks to your eyes, you have the ability to appreciate the colors of a rainbow, enjoy a smile from someone you love, or even watch out for dog poop on the sidewalk before you step in it. Your eyes are literally always looking out for you. Thanks, eyes!

How in the World Do Eyes Work?!

Have you ever noticed how difficult it is to see in the dark? Of course you have! But do you know *why?* (Uhh . . .) We'll tell you! It's because our eyes are powered by *light*. When we look at an object, light reflects or bounces off that object and enters the eye. Once that light works its way to the retina in the back of your eye, the retina turns it into signals that your brain can understand.

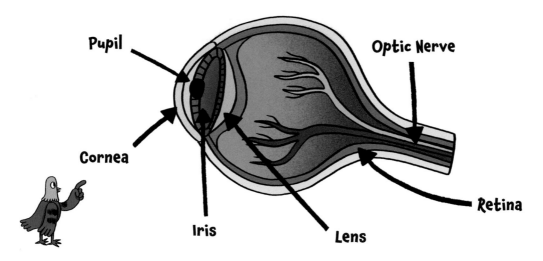

Pupil

Optic Nerve

Cornea

Retina

Iris

Lens

Putting the EYE in TEAM

Let's meet the different parts of the eye and learn a little bit about how they all work together to help you see!

Hey all! Iris here. I'm the *beautiful* colored part of your eye, and *believe it or not, I am basically all muscle!* I'm also a total control freak! It's my very important job to pick and choose the exact amount of light that's allowed to enter the lens through ol' Pupil. It's easy—I just grow and shrink, and light bends to my will. And not to toot my own horn (okay, I'm *totally tootin'* here!), but it's because of me that you can *see* in different amounts of light! If it's sunny outside, I grow extra big and put the brakes on the amount of light I allow in. And when you go to the bathroom in the middle of the night, I get *real* small, opening the gates up wide to let whatever light is out there come in. In other words, *eye* am super loyal and there for you day or night!

IRIS

Um . . . hello, my name is Cornea and I am here to protect and serve. You probably don't even notice I'm here. I'm just a thick, clear, protective layer guarding your eye from all the junk that tries to get in there. If you protect me by not sticking garbage in your eye, you can rest assured that I will always protect you. And by you, I mean your eyeball, and that's pretty much it.

CORNEA

Hi, hi! Pupil here! Some people call me "PeeOOP" and some call me "Poopil," but I prefer to be called by my given name, Pupil. I am that little black dot in the middle of your eye. Can you even imagine what your eye would look like without me?! Try it right now—IMAGINE IT! NOW STOP IMAGINING IT! Creepy, right? My job is to let the light in to hit the back part of your eye, called Retina. (*Shout-out to Retinaaaa!*) Retina and I work together like a projector and a movie screen. Like a projector, the light that comes through me is focused by Lens (you'll meet Lens next), and then it's projected onto Retina just like a movie screen! Okay, Lens, you're up!

PUPIL

Hello, my name is Lens, and like Pupil said, it's my job to keep things focused. And by "things," I mean light. I sit back here behind Iris, WHO DOESN'T EVEN KNOW I EXIST BECAUSE I'M SO CLEAR AND COLORLESS, and focus light rays on the back of your eyeball, AKA (also known as) Retina. Retina, take it away!

LENS

They call me Retina, because that's what I am. For me, every day is Opposite Day, and here's why: Because your eyeball is curved, whatever you look at hits me upside down. Even so, I take this information and send it to your brain via Optic Nerve. Thankfully, your brain has the power to flip it around and make it right-side up again. Hey, Optic Nerve! Introduce yourself!

DOWN IS UP!

RETINA

OPTIC NERVE

Nice to meet you! My name is Optic Nerve and I pretty much just hang out here at the back of your eye and send info on what you see to your brain. No biggie, I'm just the messenger. Except, of course, YOU WOULD NEVER BE ABLE TO SEE WITHOUT ME!

BOOGERS

They're Not Just for Noses!

Eye boogers are those sticky, crusty little bits of oil, mucus, ooze, and dead skin cells that clump up in the inner corners of your eyes and gross you out in the mirror. While you're awake, you're blinking them away before they're even able to set up shop. But during your blinkless sleep, they settle in, waiting to greet you in the morning!

GOOD MORNING EYE BOOGERS!

2 FOR 1 EYEBROWS

GUARANTEED TO...

- PROTECT YOUR PEEPERS FROM SWEAT AND RAIN!
- SHADE YOUR VISUAL PING-PONGS FROM THE BLAZING SUN!
- DEFLECT DIRT AND DEBRIS FROM HITTING YOUR EYEBALLS!

- HELP YOUR FACE EXPRESS A FULL RANGE OF HUMAN EMOTIONS:

HAPPINESS!   SURPRISE!   ANGER!

NOW IN A VARIETY OF SHAPES ✳ AND SIZES! ✳

EYEBROWS: GET YOURSELF A PAIR OF THE HARDEST-WORKING HAIRS ON THE HUMAN FACE!

What in the Wow?

★ The word "pupil" means "little person." Could this be because tiny versions of ourselves are reflected in other people's pupils?!

★ Due to our lack of thick fur everywhere, our furry eyebrows are much more noticeable than other animals'. But just imagine if your family pet had eyebrows as bushy as yours. A fish with eyebrows?! No laughing!!

★ There are about 250 hairs in a human eyebrow, but grownups who have never plucked them could have more than one thousand hairs!

Eyelids (AKA eyelash holders) are the official blinkers of the human face. They not only help to keep our eyeballs slimy with mucus and oils—and help to refocus our eyes when we blink—but they also work like tiny windshield wipers to clear away all the dust and other microscopic junk that shouldn't be there.

WOW DON'T YOU . . . ?

BLINK! BLANK! BLINK! BLANK!

Set your timer for one minute and count how many times you blink naturally in that time. Chances are you'll count somewhere between fifteen and twenty blinks. Do you feel like you missed anything in each tenth of a second that your eyes were closed? Probably not. But why? Turns out our brains have the amazing ability to automatically stitch together what we see between blinks, essentially filling in the blanks!

A Blink of an Eye

Newborn babies are the world champions when it comes to the art of staring competitions. Some babies blink as little as **ONCE** a minute! Grownups, on the other hand, can hardly keep their eyes open, clocking in at a whopping average of fifteen blinks a minute.

Wow-to Experiment: Host a staring-contest smackdown between a newborn baby and a grownup. Set a clock for one minute and count the blinks between the two opponents. Do you have what it takes to challenge the winner?

Fact Snacks

★ While your nose and ears continue to grow, grow, grow throughout your lifetime, the eyes that you were born with stay the same: about the size of a Ping-Pong ball! (Okay, fine. They grow a few measly millimeters in the first two years of your life, but after that, they pretty much stay the same.)

★ People with blue eyes all share a common ancestor!

★ Some people have two or even three *rows* of eyelashes! Actress Elizabeth Taylor was one of these people.

★ People with heterochromia have two different colored eyes or eyes that have more than one color. Just another reason to always look people in the irises!

GROSS!

★ When you get snotty while crying, it's a result of tears draining into the back of your nose and mixing with snot.

★ Because of blinking, our eyes are closed for about 10 percent of the time we're awake!

★ As many as 20 percent of people, from babies to adults, can sleep with their eyes open!

★ Astronauts cannot cry in space—at least not the usual way. Without gravity, tears don't fall downward out of the eye. Instead, they form into little balls of liquid that hang out *in* the eye and cause a stinging sensation. And according to astronaut Chris Hadfield, space tears can really *sting!*

RECORD-BREAKING WOW!

In 2007, **Kim Goodman** "popped" her eyeballs .47 inches (12 mm) *beyond* her eye sockets and became the Guinness World Record holder for the Farthest Eyeball Pop. Don't try this at home.

Two Whats?! and a Wow

Use your eyeballs to spot the true wow among the totally made-up whats?!:

1. If unprotected, your eyes can get sunburned.

2. If you sneeze with your eyes open, your eyeballs will pop out of your face.

3. One out of ten humans suffer from "ticklish eyes."

Quiz—The Eye Exam

1. The most common eye color in the world is . . .

    (A) Blue
    (B) Hazel
    (C) Brown
    (D) Mismatched colors

2. Eye transplants are . . .

    (A) Fun
    (B) A pain in the eye
    (C) Dangerous but worth it
    (D) Currently impossible

DADDY WANTS A NEW PAIR OF CONTACTS!

WHICH COLOR?

ANSWERS

1. (C) Brown. *Over half* of the people in the world have brown eyes.

2. (D) Currently impossible. Surgeons are unable to rewire the *one million* fibers that make up the optic nerve, which connects the eye to the brain. But, it is possible to get a cornea transplant.

NOSE

Let's Get Nosey

Nose, beak, snoot, schnozzle, hooter, sniffer, honker, schnoz, smeller, snout . . . call it what you want. Noses come in all sorts of different shapes and sizes, but always in the same place with the same purpose. Not only is it the first stop on the ol' respiratory highway, but when it comes to smell, and even taste, *the nose knows!*

So *how* do we smell? For something to be smelly, it needs to have tiny particles that fly off when you inhale. These tiny particles are called odorants, and they pass through your nose and land on different odor receptors. These odor receptors then send high-speed signals to your brain, telling you what you're smelling. You have roughly 400 different kinds of odor receptors in your nose.

When it comes to our olfactory system, taste and smell make quite the perfect pair. While many of us might credit the tongue for helping us experience taste, it's the nose that is working hard behind the scenes to make it all possible.

RECORD-BREAKING WOW!

On March 18, 2010, a Turkish man named **Mehmet Özyürek** won the Guinness World Record for the longest nose on a living person, with a schnoz measuring in at 3.46 inches (8.8 centimeters), bridge to tip!

Here's how your nose works:

Step 1: You're eating a big ice cream cone.

Step 2: The ice cream releases teeny-tiny chemicals that travel up to your nose.

Step 3: Little olfactory receptors, or sensors, in your nose wake up. Rise and shine!

Step 4: The olfactory sensors in your nose get in contact with your taste buds (*Incoming! Food odor detected!*) to create the true flavor of that ice cream cone.

Step 5: The olfactory receptors in your nose and the taste buds in your mouth send a joint message to your brain to say, "HEY BRAIN! YOU JUST ATE ICE CREAM!"

INCOMING! FOOD ODOR DETECTED!

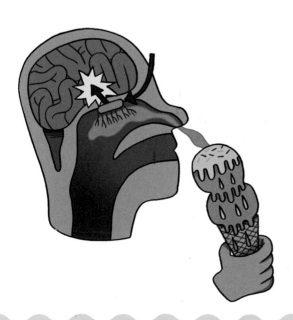

HEY BRAIN! YOU JUST ATE ICE CREAM!

17

WOW DON'T YOU . . . ?

Take a bite of food and think about how it tastes. Then take another bite of that same food, only this time pinch your nose to close your nostrils. Notice any difference?

Nostrils

Septum

Nasal Cavity

Parts of a Nose:

Nostrils—the finger-size holes in your nose. (Just because you can fit your fingers in there doesn't mean you should!)

Septum—made out of bone and cartilage, the septum is the little bendy wall between your nostrils.

Nasal cavity—this is a good kind of cavity, so please don't have it removed.

WHAT'S GOING ON DOWN THERE?

Fact Snacks

★ The floor of your nose is the roof of your mouth!

★ Your nose never stops growing!

★ Until the age of three or four months, a newborn baby can breathe only from its nose.

★ On average, men have longer noses than women.

★ In New Zealand, the Maori people have a tradition of pressing their noses together as a way of saying hi. This is known as the *hongi*.

★ Your nose makes about one quart of snot every single day, and you swallow most of it!

Why Is There Hair in My Nose?

If you've ever taken the time to examine your nose in a mirror, you might have noticed that your nostrils contain teeny-tiny hairs. They don't require shampoo, soap, or even haircuts (at least not yet), and you definitely can't braid them or pull them into a tiny nose-hair bun. So what's the point?! Why do we even have these nose hairs in the first place?

Nose hairs actually play a pretty important role in keeping you healthy. Day and night, these little hair goalies guard your nostrils, ready to trap any dirt, viruses, bacteria, and toxins that try to infiltrate your body. Sometimes you'll send these bad bits back into the universe by sneezing or by blowing your nose. Other times, they'll join forces and become . . . boogers!

Booger Recipe
- DUST
- DEAD SKIN
- POLLEN
- GERMS

Boogers (Also Known as Nasal Mucus, Which, Let's Be Honest, Is Not That Fun to Say), AKA Dehydrated Snot

Nostrils

Nostrils are also called "nares." To help you remember, pull the tip of your nose up with your finger, approach a friend or loved one, and in a panicked voice, say, *"There are hairs in my nares (NARE-eez)!"*

WE'RE HELPING!

Why do we have two nostrils (nares) instead of one? When it comes to nostrils, smelling is a team sport. At any given time, one of your nostrils is working harder than the other, creating a sort of high-flow–low-flow situation. One nostril will sniff air faster than the other while simultaneously picking up different odor chemicals than the other nostril smelling the same thing.

IS IT OKAY TO EAT MY BOOGERS?

S'NOT a big deal!

Relax! You swallow nasal mucus (snot) every time you sniffle and swallow.

Mucus that turns into boogers can also contain germs that could strengthen the immune system if ingested.

Boogers contain cavity-fighting proteins.

One small study from 1995 found that 91 percent of adults picked their noses.

"Mucophagy" is a fancy name for "eating boogers."

Could I interest you in a freshly made hambooger from the mucophagy menu?

S'NOT a good idea.

GET YOUR GERMY FINGER OUT OF YOUR NOSE! You could irritate the delicate lining of your nostrils and cause a nosebleed!

Have you ever examined a booger under a microscope? It's like a tiny dirt-filled sticky bun! Do you really want to put a dirt-filled sticky bun in your mouth?

If your hands are dirty, you're eating all the gross stuff on your fingers, too!

MINDY!!!

EARS

Hear Ye, Hear Ye!

By now you've probably figured out that those skin-covered, seashell-looking things hanging off the sides of your head are called ears. Your ears have three main parts, most of which are actually *inside* your head. These parts work together to collect sounds and send them to your brain. This is how we hear. But that's not all! For mammals like us, ears are also crucial in terms of helping our bodies stay physically balanced. Without them, we'd likely get motion sickness and flop over!

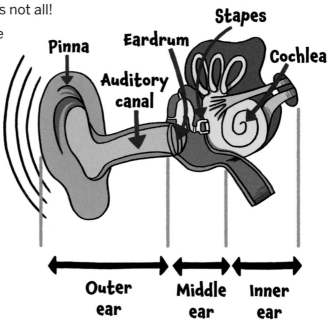

Pinna

Eardrum

Stapes

Cochlea

Auditory canal

Outer ear

Middle ear

Inner ear

WOW DON'T YOU . . . ?

Draw a Self-Portrait Replacing Your Human Ears with Ears of Corn.

EAR**ESISTIBLE**
Earbnb FOR RENT

EAR CONDITIONED!

LOOKING FOR A QUICK GETAWAY? IN SEARCH OF A PLACE FILLED WITH TRANQUIL SOUNDS AND INNER BALANCE? THEN HAVE NO FEAR. THIS SEARIOUSLY CHARMING, THREE PART Earbnb IS JUST THE EXPEARIENCE YOU'VE BEEN LOOKING FOR!

★ AN OUTER EAR COMPLETE WITH ITS OWN SOUND GATHERING PINNA! AS YOU'LL SEE, THE PINNA IS MADE OF CARTILAGE COVERED IN LUXURIOUSLY SOFT SKIN. (OOH LA LA!) IN ADDITION TO THE PINNA, THE OUTER EAR ALSO FEATURES ITS OWN ROBUST ONE-INCH (2.5-CM) CANAL THAT RUNS THROUGH THE MIDDLE EAR, LEADING TO ITS VERY OWN EARDRUM.

THE OUTER EAR

★ GOOD VIBES! INSIDE THIS SPACIOUS, AIR-FILLED MIDDLE EAR CAVITY, EXPERIENCE SOOTHING SOUND WAVES TURNED INTO VIBRATIONS AS THEY BOUNCE OFF THIS STATE-OF-THE-ART EARDRUM!

THE MIDDLE EAR CAVITY

★ THIS INNER EAR IS WHERE ALL THE MAGIC HAPPENS. INSIDE, YOU'LL FIND NOT ONLY A SENSE OF INNER BALANCE, BUT ALSO A VARIETY OF WALL-TO-WALL VIBRATIONS TURNED INTO UP-TO-THE-MINUTE MESSAGING SIGNALS AND SENT STRAIGHT TO YOUR BRAIN (A DELIVERY OF TINY INVISIBLE AUDITORY POSTCARDS!)

THE INNER EAR

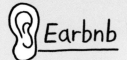Earbnb

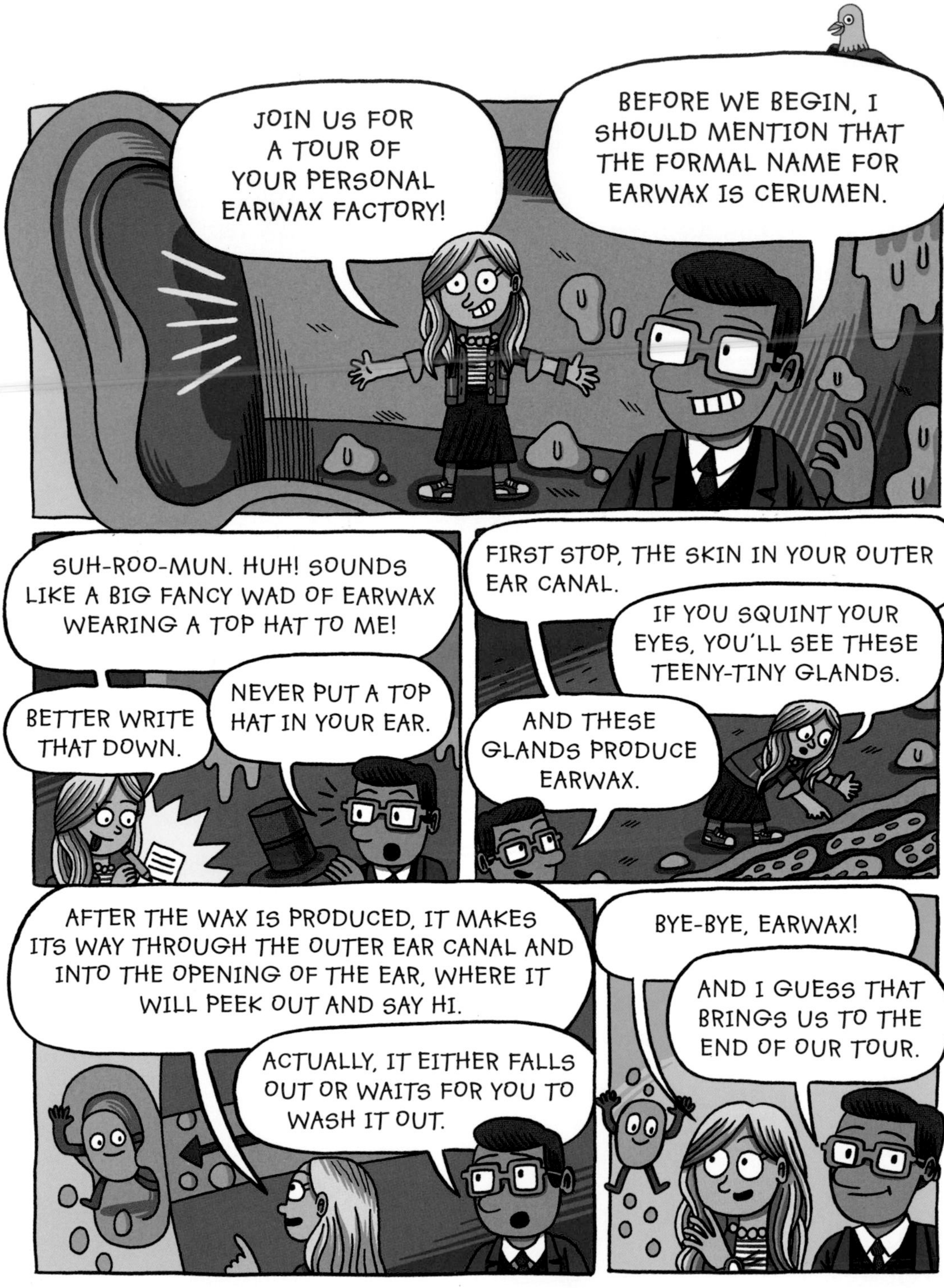
JOIN US FOR A TOUR OF YOUR PERSONAL EARWAX FACTORY!
BEFORE WE BEGIN, I SHOULD MENTION THAT THE FORMAL NAME FOR EARWAX IS CERUMEN.
SUH-ROO-MUN. HUH! SOUNDS LIKE A BIG FANCY WAD OF EARWAX WEARING A TOP HAT TO ME!
BETTER WRITE THAT DOWN.
NEVER PUT A TOP HAT IN YOUR EAR.
FIRST STOP, THE SKIN IN YOUR OUTER EAR CANAL.
IF YOU SQUINT YOUR EYES, YOU'LL SEE THESE TEENY-TINY GLANDS.
AND THESE GLANDS PRODUCE EARWAX.
AFTER THE WAX IS PRODUCED, IT MAKES ITS WAY THROUGH THE OUTER EAR CANAL AND INTO THE OPENING OF THE EAR, WHERE IT WILL PEEK OUT AND SAY HI.
ACTUALLY, IT EITHER FALLS OUT OR WAITS FOR YOU TO WASH IT OUT.
BYE-BYE, EARWAX!
AND I GUESS THAT BRINGS US TO THE END OF OUR TOUR.

Why Do We Have Earwax, Anyway?

Earwax is the first line of defense against invaders like dirt and bacteria that try to work their way in through our ears. Depending on the person, earwax can be sticky, dry, or drippy, and it can range from a light yellow to a dark orange. Earwax comes in all sorts of varieties.

In a battle for the world's juiciest earwax, the award goes to . . . KIDS! Kids have wetter earwax than grownups.

RECORD-BREAKING WOW!

In 2007, Anthony Victor, a retired principal from Madurai, India, won the Guinness World Record for Longest Ear Hair. How long was it? Growing from the center of his outer ears, the "Ear-Haired Teacher" had a tuft of hair measuring 7.12 inches (18.1 cm) long. That's almost as long as a pencil! With ear hair that long, how would you style it?

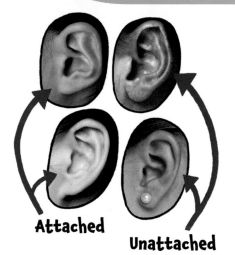

Attached

Unattached

Earlobes

All people have earlobes, but how they're attached is determined by several genes in the person they're attached to! Take some time to notice the differences in the earlobes of your friends and family. Are they dangly? Are they completely attached? What earlobe style do you find most common among the people you know?

Fact Snacks

★ Our ancient human ancestors might have been able to hear better at higher frequencies than we can today.

★ Your voice sounds lower to you than it does to the person you're talking to.

★ Some people have a hearing sensitivity that allows them to hear their own eyeballs moving around in their sockets!

★ Do your ears hang low? Do they wobble to and fro? Can you tie them in a knot? Can you tie them in a bow? Well, the answer is . . . um . . . eventually? Just like your nose, your outer ears are made of cartilage, and they never stop growing!

What in the Wow?

It's been estimated that 10 to 20 percent of humans can wiggle their own ears! And of those people, some just can't stop wiggling. There's a condition known as moving ear syndrome.

I CAN'T DO IT!

WOW TIP

Things you should never put in your ears: corn, batteries, small fish, or really anything smaller than your elbow. But you can go hog-wild on putting your elbows in your ears. Try it! Just keep your elbows out of other people's ears. It's bad manners.

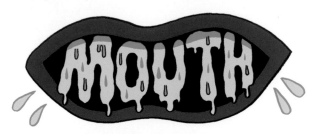

The Biggest Hole in the Human Head

The mouth is defined as "the opening in the lower part of the human face, surrounded by the lips, through which food is taken in and from which speech and other sounds are emitted."

Wow! That's a big mouthful of words to swallow. Let's break it down.

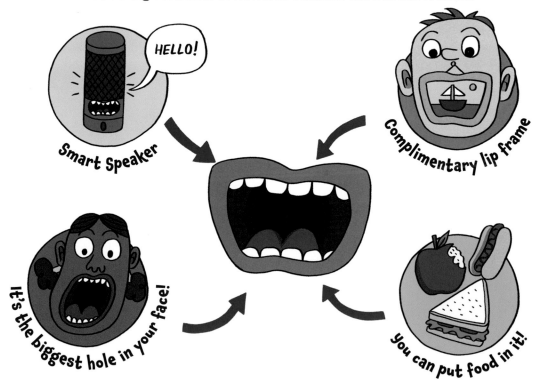

Smart Speaker

HELLO!

Complimentary lip frame

It's the biggest hole in your face!

You can put food in it!

Are you sold? *Yay!* Let us introduce you to . . . *your mouth.*

Teeth

Ah, teeth. The little white picket fences of the mouth. Teeth help us to smile, speak, and most importantly, chew our food. And lucky for us humans, we get two full sets of them in our lifetimes.

Kids start off with twenty "milk" teeth, also known as baby teeth. They're tiny, shiny, and white and first pop through our gums at around six months old, causing our grownups to notify relatives, alert the local news, and shriek with delight.

But those baby teeth won't be around for long. In fact, by the time we're seven or eight years old, those teeth start jumping out of our mouths to make way for a new set of chompers to come barreling through our gums. These are your adult teeth. All

thirty-two of them are bigger, yellower, harder, and here to stay. These adult teeth can tear apart a T-bone steak, gnaw their way through a tough piece of asparagus, and rip a price tag off a new shirt (even though that is *not* what they are made for). Let's take a moment to get to know our teeth. Open wide!

I like my baby teeth. Why do I have to "lose" them?

Losing our baby teeth is just another part of growing up! As babies and kids, our mouths are just not big enough for thirty-two adult-size teeth, so our baby teeth serve as little placeholders until our mouths grow big enough for the big dogs to erupt.

So then why do I need adult teeth at all? Why can't I just keep my baby teeth in my mouth forever?

Why?! Because it would look something like this:

AHHHHHHHHHHHHHHHHHHHHHHHHHHHHHHH!!!

You get it now?

AAHHHHHHHHHHHHHHHHHHH-HHHHHHHHHHHHHH!!

Your mouth is home to three different types of teeth: incisors, canines, and molars. Each of these teeth has a different job to do, and unless you are one of those people who enjoys eating in front of a mirror while chewing with your mouth open (hey, we're not here to judge!), you might be living with these teeth and not even realizing what they're doing for you at every meal.

Incisors These are the attention-grabbing teeth at the front of your mouth. They are smooth on the bottom, but sharp enough to cut through a carrot in a single bite. *And* you get eight of them!

Canines These are those little fang teeth that sit in the corners of your mouth. They are sharp, pointy, and good for gripping food and tearing it to shreds. Pay attention to your canine teeth the next time you eat some overcooked chicken or the tough end of a green bean. Those four canines will show your food who's boss!

Molars These are the teeth found in the back of your mouth that look like three or four teeth in one. Compared to the showstoppers sitting pretty in the front of your mouth, these babies are *big*. They're also super reliable. Your molars help to *chew*, *crush*, and *grind* your food. Without molars, eating would feel super weird. If you don't believe us, try chewing an apple using only your incisors and canines.

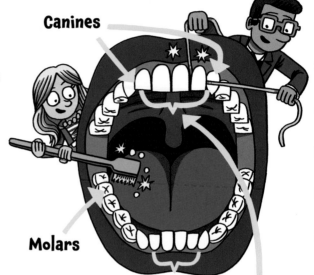

Canines

Molars

Incisors

Jokes Grownups Love to Make
Oh, you lost your tooth, huh? Well, ya better go find it!

The part of the tooth that you can see is called the crown. The crown is covered in a shiny coating called enamel. Enamel, made mostly out of minerals, is the hardest substance in the whole human body. And since it does not contain any living cells, your body can't make any more of it. So when it comes to your teeth, it's best to treat your crowns like royalty!

YOUR HIGHNESS, I WOULD LIKE TO PRESENT YOU WITH YOUR TOOTHBRUSH AND TOOTHPASTE.

What in the Wow?

★ Most mammals (including humans) have two sets of teeth throughout our lifetime. Because of this, we are known as "diphyodont."

★ Alligators will regrow teeth in the same tooth socket up to fifty times in a lifetime. (Alligators have terrible oral hygiene!)

★ Some animals—like sharks, crocs, elephants, and kangaroos—lose and grow teeth over and over again throughout their lives. Because of this, these animals are known as "polyphyodont."

Diphyodont

Polyphyodont

HEY! I BRUSH MY TEETH! HONEST!

DON'T WORRY ABOUT ME! I'VE GOT PLENTY MORE TEETH TO GROW BACK!

DON'T WORRY, THEY'LL GROW BACK!

CAVITY CRAFT CORNER

WELCOME. TODAY, WE'RE GOING TO SHOW YOU HOW TO MAKE YOUR OWN CAVITY. "CAVITY" IS JUST A FUN NAME FOR "GAPING HOLE IN YOUR TOOTH THAT DEFINITELY SHOULD NOT BE THERE AND MIGHT CAUSE YOU PAIN."

DON'T TRY THIS AT HOME!

1 THE FIRST THING YOU'RE GOING TO NEED IS A BUNCH OF SUGAR.

2 NEXT, YOU ARE GOING TO TAKE THIS SUGAR AND FEED IT TO THE BACTERIA IN YOUR MOUTH. EASY DOES IT... NOT TOO FAST... AH, JUST DUMP IT IN!

DID YOU KNOW THAT YOU HAVE OVER THREE HUNDRED SPECIES OF BACTERIA LIVING IN YOUR MOUTH? AND OVER A BILLION AT ANY ONE TIME? SOME OF THIS BACTERIA IS GOOD FOR US, BUT THAT'S NOT THE BACTERIA WE'RE USING TO MAKE OUR CAVITY TODAY.

BY FEEDING SUGAR TO THE BAD BACTERIA, WE ARE HELPING IT TO FORM SOMETHING CALLED DENTAL PLAQUE. DENTAL PLAQUE IS THE SLIMY, COLORLESS GRIME THAT COATS OUR TEETH.

AFTER A LITTLE WHILE, IT HARDENS, TAKING UP PERMANENT RESIDENCE UNTIL A DENTIST COMES ALONG TO CHIP IT AWAY. BUT NOT TODAY!

3 TODAY WE ARE GOING TO WAIT FOR THE BACTERIA TO EAT THE SUGAR, AND ALONG WITH IT, THE PROTECTIVE ENAMEL ON YOUR TEETH. AND WHILE WE'RE WAITING FOR THIS TO HAPPEN, WE'RE JUST GOING TO WAIT...

AND WAIT... AND DON'T EVEN THINK ABOUT BRUSHING YOUR TEETH.

NOM NOM NOM!

4 AND... DING! THAT SHOULD DO IT. LET'S CHECK THAT TOOTH.

WHILE WE WERE WAITING, A TINY, DARK, AND STICKY HOLE WAS FORMING IN YOUR TOOTH!

CONGRATURITOS! YOU JUST MADE YOUR VERY OWN CAVITY!

SHARE THE WOW

The next time you bust your grandparents in a ten-second smooch, remind them that they are spreading over eighty million bacteria between their mouths. And probably a little bit of spinach too. *Eww.*

Fact Snacks

★ Just like fingerprints, no two teeth are exactly alike.

★ About a third of each tooth lives under your gum. Take good care of your gums and your gums will take good care of your teeth.

Tooth under gum

★ Your body makes almost 7,000 gallons (26,280 L) of spit over a lifetime. That's enough spit to fill two bathtubs a year! Spit bath, anyone?

YUCK!

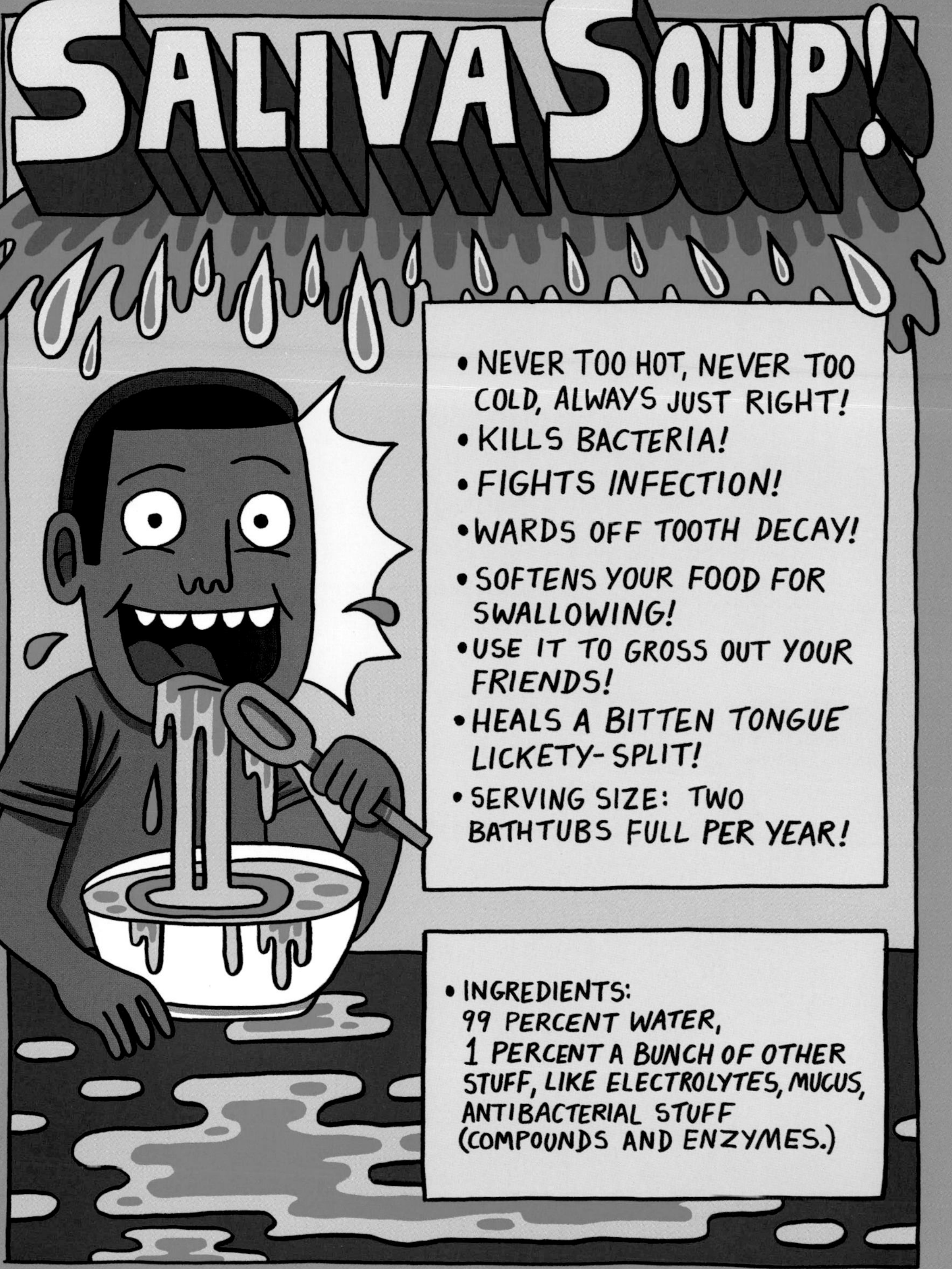
SALIVA SOUP!
• NEVER TOO HOT, NEVER TOO COLD, ALWAYS JUST RIGHT!
• KILLS BACTERIA!
• FIGHTS INFECTION!
• WARDS OFF TOOTH DECAY!
• SOFTENS YOUR FOOD FOR SWALLOWING!
• USE IT TO GROSS OUT YOUR FRIENDS!
• HEALS A BITTEN TONGUE LICKETY-SPLIT!
• SERVING SIZE: TWO BATHTUBS FULL PER YEAR!
• INGREDIENTS:
99 PERCENT WATER,
1 PERCENT A BUNCH OF OTHER STUFF, LIKE ELECTROLYTES, MUCUS, ANTIBACTERIAL STUFF (COMPOUNDS AND ENZYMES.)

The Tongue

The tongue is a muscular organ in the mouth that helps us to chew, swallow, taste, and speak. (Thanks, tongue!) Most tongues are about three inches (7.6 cm) long and covered in a thin layer of moist, pink tissue called mucosa, tiny bumps called papillae, and of course, our taste buds.

Tongue Twisting

Taco tongue

Tongue rolling, or taco tongue, is at least partially genetic. If one of your parents can do it, there's a pretty good chance that you can too. Try it and see for yourself.

Four-leaf clover

Considered to be the trickiest type of tongue twisting, the four-leaf clover is formed when a person is able to fold their tongue into multiple bends that resemble a four-leaf clover.

Tongue turning

This tricky tongue technique is accomplished by twisting the edges of the tongue to face sideways.

"Pad kid poured curd pulled cold"

In 2013, researchers from the Massachusetts Institute of Technology named this the world's toughest tongue twister!

What in the Wow?

★ Only 10 percent of people worldwide can touch their nose with their tongue! Are *you* one of them?

★ For centuries, the people of Tibet have greeted one another by sticking out their tongues.

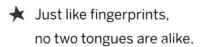

★ Just like fingerprints, no two tongues are alike.

RECORD-BREAKING WOW!

Ashish Peri, of Mumbai, India, is the first and only world record holder for Most Tongue to Nose Touches in One Minute. That's 142 touches in 60 seconds!

Thomas Blackstone, of the UK, once used his tongue to lift a weight of 24 pounds, 3 ounces (10.9 kg) and won the record for Heaviest Weight Lifted by Tongue.

Blue whales, the largest animals on Earth, also have the world's largest tongue. Weighing in at 5,400 pounds (2,500 kg), the blue whale's tongue is as heavy as an elephant!

Taste Buds

Ah, taste buds. Or should we call them taste *buddies?* Always there for us through not only the sweet and savory times but the sour and bitter times too. Birthday cakes, french fries, lemon drops, and onion cries, our taste buds are there to help determine how we feel about the foods we eat.

So what are taste buds, anyway? Find a mirror and stick out your tongue. See those little bumps? Those bumps are called papillae. Most of those papillae bumps contain *tiny* taste buds covered in even tinier hairs called microvilli (my-kro-VILL-eye). And like a personal postal service, those teeny-tiny hairs are responsible for sending messages to your brain to tell you how something tastes.

Microvilli

Taste Buds

Papillae

Tongue

Classes of Flavor

Sweet tastes are mostly caused by something you're probably not *at all* familiar with, a food substance commonly known as sugar. (*What?* You've heard of it?!) Sugar is found in everything from fruit, maple syrup, and honey to chocolate cake, candy, and even baked beans.

WHERE IS THAT SUGAR HIDING?

In fact, sugar seems to have worked its way into more foods than we even realize: bread, salad dressing, barbecue sauce, peanut butter, and spaghetti sauce all often contain that sneaky sugar.

WOW DON'T YOU . . . ?

Check the food labels in your refrigerator and pantry and seek surprising spots where sugar might be hiding.

Sour tastes are caused by acid. You may recognize these sour-tasting acids in lemons, vinegar, and fermented foods like sauerkraut. But what does sour taste like? Well, we could *tell* you, but we'd rather *show* you. Try licking a sour fruit like a lemon while you look at your reflection in a mirror. If the taste causes you to make a face by scrunching up your mouth and squinting your eyes, you'll know you've experienced a serious sour sensation.

WOW DON'T YOU . . . ?

Have a sour food taste challenge: taste three different sour foods and try not to make a sour face to match.

Bitter tastes have a sharp, powerful bite that might take a little getting used to. Uncooked kale, brussels sprouts, and pure chocolate/cocoa are all examples of crazy-bitter foods. We taste bitter flavors near the backs of our tongues more intensely. Scientists believe that our ancestors used this trait to help avoid bitter plants, which could be a sign that they were poisonous or rotten. Today, we humans sometimes still feel the urge to spit out foods that taste extra bitter to us.

Salty tastes . . . salty! That saltiness comes from a chemical called sodium chloride. (Please pass the sodium chloride!)

Umami, or as we say it, "OoOOoooOOOh MOMMYYY" (ahem!), is a type of savory taste sensation found in many Asian foods. You may recognize it in foods like seaweed, soy sauce, and Chinese cabbage. Other examples of umami can be found in cured meats, stinky cheeses, mushrooms, and broths. In Japanese, umami means "pleasant savory taste."

OOOOOH MOMMYYY!

Spiced OUT!

"Spicy" is actually not a flavor at all. In fact, your body detects the spiciness of hot peppers in the same way it detects the heat from a sip of hot cocoa.

Spicy foods like hot peppers are filled with a teeny-tiny molecule called capsaicin. Pain receptors on your lips, mouth, and tongue are tricked by the capsaicin and send heat signals to your brain.

(Attention, Mission Control: it appears that we are about to be SPICED OUT.)

Here's how it works:

Step 1: You confidently and unwittingly take a bite of a hot pepper.

Step 2: Pain receptors on your lips, mouth, and tongue are all greeted by the capsaicin hiding inside the pepper.

Step 3: The pain receptors send emergency signals to your brain that say, *"We have been spiced out!"*

Step 4: The rest of your body comes to the rescue in embarrassing ways in an attempt to cool you down and chill you out. This can involve excessive sweating, a runny nose, and watery eyes. Or in extreme cases, all three!

Do You Have What It Takes to Be a SUPERTASTER?

Are you a human person who tastes flavors *way* more intensely than your friends? Do you find desserts too sweet and veggies too bitter to bite? Are you easily spiced out?

If you answered yes to these three questions, you might be . . . a SUPERTASTER. Supertasters have more taste buds than the average human and something going on in their brains that even scientists still don't fully understand.

Linda Bartoshuk at the University of Florida accidentally discovered supertasters back in the 1990s while studying something called taste blindness. Taste blindness happens when a person goes "blind" to certain flavors. Bartoshuk was comparing whether taste-blind people could taste a bitter flavor as intensely as typical tasters, but found that a third of the people in her experiment tasted bitterness a lot more than others.

BABY BODY PARTS

While it's been years since your body was a baby, your body itself is chock-full of new life. Allow us to introduce you to your body's newest additions. These parts come and go without you even noticing, renewing themselves constantly!

 ## Mucosa

NICKNAME: Stomach Lining

AGE: Five days old

DETAILS: Already knows how to help digest food.

☆ Taste Buds

AGE: Ten days old

DETAILS: Available to help you experience the taste of food. Specializes in sensing the tastes of sweet, salty, sour, bitter, and umami.

Epidermis

NICKNAME: Skin Cells (the top layer)

AGE: Two weeks old

DETAILS: A little flaky. Only expected to stick around for another two weeks. Easily replaceable.

Eyelashes

AGE: Two months old

DETAILS: Born ready to shield your eyes from danger. Dust and dirt particles don't stand a chance against these batty babies. Pretty short expected lifespan, but you'll hardly notice when they're gone.

Red Blood Cells

AGE: Four months old

DETAILS: Thrive in your blood. Tiny cells, big helpers! Ready to deliver oxygen and remove trash from other cells.

THE BRAIN

It's What Makes Up
Your Mind!

THE BRAIN

It's What Makes Up Your Mind!

The brain is mission control to the entire human body—a virtual computer operating from within your skull, commanding every movement, every thought, every memory, and every emotion. Even while you sleep! It's powerful, it's bossy, it's spongy, *and* it's the most complex organ of your entire body.

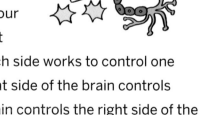

The brain contains billions of teeny-tiny nerve cells called neurons that act like messengers, sending information to and from the brain and the rest of your body. It is divided into two hemispheres, or sides. It gets pretty complicated, but for the most part, each side works to control one half the body. But (and this is a BIG BUTT), the right side of the brain controls the left side of the body, and the left side of the brain controls the right side of the body. Let's take a tour!

SCRAMBLED SENSES

Some people have a condition known as synesthesia. With synesthesia, a sense like smell might activate another sense, like sight—at the same time! A person with synesthesia might hear colors, taste shapes, or feel sounds. *Wow! This song tastes like chicken!*

Map of the Human Brain

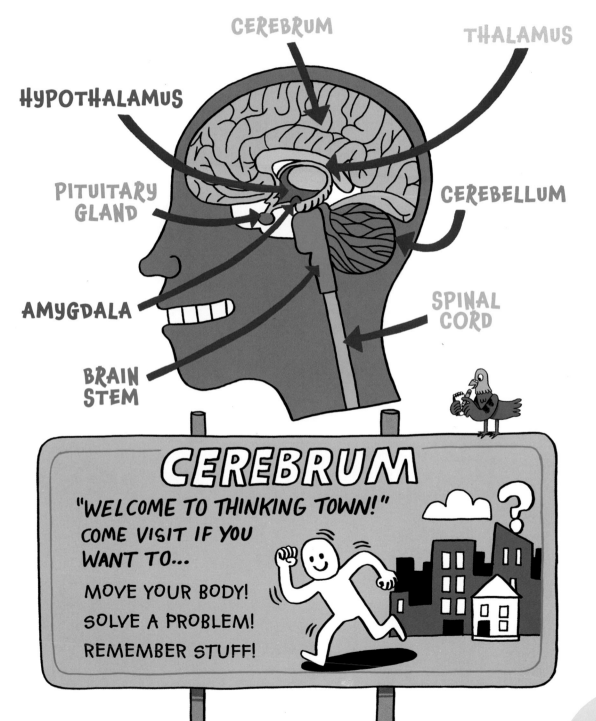

CEREBRUM

THALAMUS

HYPOTHALAMUS

PITUITARY GLAND

CEREBELLUM

AMYGDALA

SPINAL CORD

BRAIN STEM

CEREBRUM

"WELCOME TO THINKING TOWN!"
COME VISIT IF YOU WANT TO...

MOVE YOUR BODY!

SOLVE A PROBLEM!

REMEMBER STUFF!

THALAMUS
SENSORY CITY!

VISIT US FOR ALL YOUR TOUCHY-FEELY NEEDS. WE TAKE AND PROCESS INFORMATION FROM YOUR FIVE SENSES.

HYPOTHALAMUS

COME ON DOWN TO TEMPERATURE TOWN!

LOOKING TO CONTROL YOUR BODY'S TEMPERATURE? WELL, YOU'VE COME TO THE RIGHT PLACE. WE'VE GOT THE SHIVERS AND THE SWEATS TO KEEP YOUR BODY COOKIN' AT AROUND A COMFORTABLE 98.6 DEGREES FAHRENHEIT (37 DEGREES C)!

 EAT, DRINK, SLEEP, REPEAT.

WE KEEP TRACK OF ALL YOUR THIRST, HUNGER, AND SLEEP NEEDS. VISIT US FOR PERSONAL ALERTS!

PITUITARY GLAND
YOUR NEIGHBORHOOD PEA BRAIN!

COME VISIT US IF YOU'RE LOOKING TO GROW!

IF YOU LIVED HERE, YOU'D BE **BIG** BY NOW.

What?!

It's the size of a pea, but it's famous for helping bodies grow.

CEREBELLUM

THE TINY BUTT OF THE BRAIN

COME VISIT IF YOU'RE IN SEARCH OF:

INNER BALANCE

COORDINATION

SMOOTH MOVES

No one calls it this.

I DO!

BRAIN STEM

KEEPING BODIES ALIVE 365!

COME SEE US IF YOU ENJOY ACTIVITIES SUCH AS . . .

BREATHING

DIGESTING FOOD

HAVING A HEARTBEAT

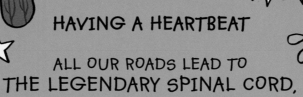

ALL OUR ROADS LEAD TO
THE LEGENDARY SPINAL CORD,
WHERE MAIL CARRIERS ARE STANDING BY TO SORT
THROUGH THE MILLIONS OF MESSAGES SENT
BACK AND FORTH BETWEEN THE BRAIN AND
THE REST OF YOUR BODY.

⚡ SPINAL CORD ⚡
✉ ⌗ YOU'VE GOT MAIL! ⌗ ✉

AS YOUR PERSONAL POSTAL SERVICE, WE WILL DELIVER MESSAGES TO AND FROM YOUR BRAIN AND YOUR BODY FASTER THAN YOU CAN LICK A STAMP.

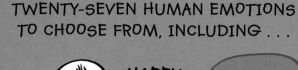

☺ AMYGDALA 😢
WE GOT THE FEELS!

TWENTY-SEVEN HUMAN EMOTIONS TO CHOOSE FROM, INCLUDING . . .

HAPPY

SAD

SCARED

ANGRY

SURPRISED

DISGUSTED

Feels? What are feels?

Feelings, Guy Raz! Emotions!

A Fully Functioning Brain Is a Team Effort

MY NAME IS **FRONTAL LOBE**, AND I'M PRETTY MUCH IN CHARGE OF ALL COMPLEX THINKING, LIKE PLANNING, IMAGINING, DECISION-MAKING, AND PROBLEM-SOLVING.

UM, YEAH . . . I'M **PARIETAL LOBE** AND I'M HERE TO HELP YOU FEEL THINGS LIKE TOUCH, PAIN, AND PRESSURE. I ALSO STEP IN IF YOU'RE ABOUT TO BURN THE ROOF OF YOUR MOUTH ON A HOT SLICE OF PIZZA. BUT DO YOU EVER LISTEN TO ME?! ASK THE ROOF OF YOUR MOUTH!

HEY THERE! I'M **OCCIPITAL LOBE**, AND PEOPLE SAY THAT I'M A BIT OF A VISIONARY. MOSTLY BECAUSE I PROCESS LIGHT AND HELP YOU SEE.

DID SOMEBODY CALL MY NAME? I'M **TEMPORAL LOBE**. I PROCESS EVERY SOUND AND EVERY WORD THAT ENTERS THE EAR. I'M GOOD AT HELPING YOU FIND YOUR MEMORIES.

THE NAME'S **CEREBELLUM**, AND WITHOUT ME, YOU WOULD FALL OVER. I HELP YOU WITH FINE MOVEMENTS AND BALANCE.

Fact Snacks

★ The average adult brain weighs three pounds (1.4 kg). That's about as much as:

A bag of onions

A pair of boots

A two-slice toaster

(Imagine what your skull would be shaped like if any of these other three-pounders took the place of your brain.)

★ A newborn baby's brain grows 1 percent larger each day until the infant's about three months old.

★ The human brain is more than three times as big as the brains of other mammals of similar size.

★ By the time you turn nine years old, your brain will be around 95 percent of the size of a grownup's brain, yet you *still* can't drive a car. What's up with that?!

★ While your brain only makes up about 2 percent of your body weight, it uses 20 percent of your daily energy supply. That's a lot of energy spent sending and receiving billions of messages in a single day!

★ The brain can store as much information as *one million* hours of TV shows!

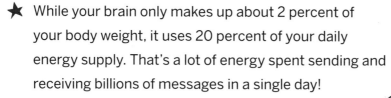

★ The human brain is as big as the whole internet! While your brain might have the storage capacity to hold the entire internet, it's limited by how quickly it can store facts and memories.

★ You have at least one thousand times more neural connections in your brain than there are stars in the galaxy. A neural connection is made when one neuron or nerve cell sends an electrical message to another neuron—sometimes all the way from one part of your body to another.

AAH, ANOTHER SATISFYING NEURAL CONNECTION

★ Pain signals to the brain can travel at speeds of up to 270 miles per hour (435 kmph). That's four times *faster* than a car travels on a highway!

★ Your brain is constantly active, using energy even while you sleep. During rest, your brain is organizing your experiences, thoughts, and memories so that you can easily access them later when you need them! Are *you* as organized as your brain?

★ A 2015 study found that ultramarathon runners' brains shrank by 6 percent during a 2,796-mile (4,500-km) race. The good news is that after six months, their brains experienced a complete bounce back to their normal size.

★ If you could smooth out all the wrinkles in your brain, it would flatten out to the size of a small pillowcase. DO NOT TRY THIS AT HOME.

BELLY BUTTONS

HELP! When I press my belly button, nothing happens!

Good news! Sounds like your belly button is doing exactly what it's supposed to do: nothing!

Huh?

Your belly button is just a scar! A scar left over from where your umbilical cord once was.

But I thought I was cordless!

You might be cordless now, but back in the day, when you were growing inside your birth mother's womb, your umbilical cord was how she was able to send oxygen and nutrients from her body to yours.

Aw, thanks, Mom! Did I send anything back to her?

You sure did! You sent her all the waste your growing body didn't need.

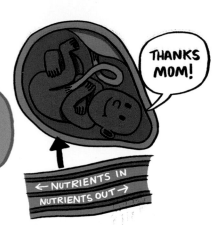

THANKS MOM!

← NUTRIENTS IN
NUTRIENTS OUT →

And what did she do with it?

Welp, she pretty much just pooped it out.

SHE WHAT?!

It's not as gross as it sounds. In fact, she couldn't even tell the difference between your waste and hers.

Whew! So what happened to my umbilical cord?

Once you were born, it basically just fell off. Your body didn't need it anymore.

Did my mom keep it?

You'll have to ask your mom.

MOM!! WHAT DID YOU DO WITH MY UMBILICAL CORD?!

I think my work here is done.

FROM THE OUTSIDE IN

Skin
It's What Keeps Your Insides In!

Sweat
Eww! What's That Smell?

Nails
Nailed It!

Hair
The Long and Short of It

 S.K.I.N:

It's What Keeps Your Insides In!

Skin (AKA your birthday suit) is the largest organ of your entire body. It weighs about as much as a newborn baby (eight pounds [3.6 kg]). If a grownup took off their birthday suit and spread it out (*gross!*), it would measure about twenty-two square feet (2 m^2), taking up half of a Ping-Pong table. (Grownups: *Do not* try this at home. Or your friend's home. Or anywhere.)

Where does skin get its color?

The color of your skin is determined by the amount of melanin you have in it. Melanin is a natural pigment or color, and it affects the eye, hair, and skin color of all humans. The more melanin in your body, the darker your skin; the less melanin in your body, the lighter your skin.

Freckles and moles appear in spots with lots of extra melanin in the skin. Newborn babies don't have freckles because they haven't been exposed to the sun long enough for them to develop.

SKIN WANTED!

DO YOU HAVE WHAT IT TAKES TO PROTECT INSIDES FROM THE OUTSIDE WORLD?

- ARE YOU OFTEN REFERRED TO AS "TOUGH" YET "STRETCHY"?

- CAN YOU STOP INNER BODILY FLUIDS FROM SPILLING OUT ALL OVER THE PLACE?

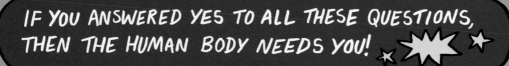

- ARE YOU WILLING TO FIGHT DISEASE AND GERM INVASIONS? TAKE OUT THE TRASH? KEEP IT COOL WHEN IT'S HOT, AND HOT WHEN IT'S COOL?

- OKAY NOT GETTING PAID FOR YOUR WORK?

IF YOU ANSWERED YES TO ALL THESE QUESTIONS, THEN THE HUMAN BODY NEEDS YOU!

- MUST BE AVAILABLE 24/7. NO TIME OFF FOR WEEKENDS AND HOLIDAYS.

* SMALL PRINT: MUST WORK WELL WITH OTHERS. AND BY "OTHERS" WE MEAN THE OTHER DEPARTMENTS OF THE HUMAN BODY, INCLUDING, BUT NOT LIMITED TO: THE DIGESTIVE, CIRCULATORY, AND NERVOUS SYSTEMS.

★ APPLY WITHIN! ★

Much like a three-layer cake, or a three-layer dip, your skin is also made up of three layers. Unlike a cake or a dip, it doesn't taste delicious. If you don't believe us, try licking your own elbow, and report back.

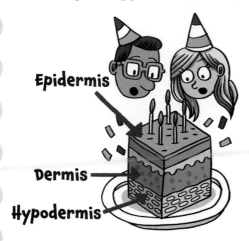

Epidermis

Dermis

Hypodermis

The top layer of your skin is what's known as the *epidermis*. It's waterproof, and it's the only layer we can see. In fact, the epidermis is where our skin color is created.

Underneath the epidermis is the layer we call the *dermis*. The dermis is where your hair and sweat make their way onto your body.

And the third and deepest layer is the *hypodermis,* or subcutis. This layer is made mostly of fat and the tissue that protects and pads your muscles and bones while attaching them to your skin. And on top of all that, it stores energy *and* helps to keep your body temperature in check.

Fact Snacks

★ Skin is like a raincoat for your guts—completely waterproof! You can stand in a rainstorm, jump in the ocean, or splash in a puddle and none of that water will be able to work its way in. But you'll still get wet!

JUST LIKE NEW!

★ Mark your calendar: by this time next month, you will have an entirely new layer of skin. Skin is your fastest-growing organ.

★ Without skin, we would literally evaporate into thin air.

★ Our bodies are constantly shedding skin cells. And if we were to save up all of these dead skin cells for an entire year, we would be lugging around a *nine-pound* (4-kg) bucket of dead skin!

★ Your body's dead skin cells feed about a million dust mites every single day. Dust mite mouths are designed like tiny chopsticks, and they grab these protein-packed flakes of skin to snack on like teeny-tiny potato chips! If your dead skin cells had a flavor, what would it be?

★ The thickest skin on your body is found on your feet. The thinnest skin on the body is found on your eyelids. Now imagine doing a skin swap in these two areas. Do not imagine this while you're eating. And don't read this out loud while someone else is eating.

RECORD-BREAKING WOW!

In 1999, **Gary Turner,** of the UK, set the Guinness World Record for the World's Stretchiest Skin. His skin is so stretchy that he's able to cover his entire lower jaw with the skin from his neck.

The Bumps

PIMPLES! (AKA ZITS, ERUPTIONS, PUSTULES, ACNE)

What are they? Pimples are small, angry bumps on the surface of your skin that first show up between the ages of twelve and seventeen. Their stay is temporary, but they often bring friends, thus turning your face into a little pimple party.

What are they made of? Think of pimples as being first planted in your pores, those tiny holes in your skin. Inside each of those pores is a mixture of oil, dead skin cells, and bacteria. (Is this making you hungry?) And this is not a bad thing. *But*, when there's too much oil, which is often the case with teenagers, that oil, dead skin, and bacteria join together to clog up your pore, rise to the surface, and before you know it, a pimple has bloomed!

MOLES!

What are they? Moles are pigmented or colored spots, marks, or bumps that may appear on your skin as the result of a buildup of skin-color cells known as melanocytes. As an involuntary member of the Mole Patrol, you will most certainly find a few in your lifetime, with most making their first appearance when you're a kid or a teenager. Moles can be flat, bumpy, smooth, lumpy, and sometimes even hairy. And while most moles are completely normal, some can make you sick, so to keep the not-so-normal moles from popping up, be sure to protect your skin from the sun.

WARTS!

What are they? Warts are small, hard, grayish-brown bumps that can pop up on your skin as the result of a virus. Sometimes they look like little bits of cauliflower covered in tiny black dots.

How do I kick a wart off my skin? Warts often go away on their own, but sometimes this can take months or even years. If a wart is painful or just too annoying to live with, you and your grownup may want to visit a doctor. Most pediatricians come equipped with wart-busting powers. (Fact: You cannot get a wart from touching a toad.)

ECZEMA! (AKA DERMATITIS)

What is it? Eczema is a red, bumpy, flaky, itchy patch that can pop up on your skin when your skin is extra sensitive to certain allergens in the environment. Pet dander, dust, soaps, sweat, scratchy clothes, and certain foods can all cause your skin to go bonkerballs, eczema-style. Eczema seems to be genetic, meaning that it's often passed from generation to generation, but not from friend to friend.

BIRTHMARKS!

What are they? Birthmarks are colored marks that develop either on or under your skin. They are caused by extra pigment-producing cells or blood vessels that decide to do their own thing. Despite the name "birthmark," they can show up before or after a baby is born. Many birthmarks will fade as you get older, while others grow more noticeable in size or color. No two birthmarks are alike, so if you have one, think of it as your trademark! Just another way your body makes you unique.

Scrapes, Scars, Scabs & Bruises, and What in the World Is That Stuff that Oozes?

Abrasion! (BUT MOST PEOPLE JUST CALL ME "SCRAPE")

FAVE HANGOUT SPOT: You can usually find me on a patch of soft skin that's had a rough surprise meeting with a sidewalk or something.

LIKES: Knees, elbows, feet, and hands are my jams.

HOW I LIKE TO BE TREATED: I'm simple. Just treat me with plenty of soap and water and I won't give you any trouble.

Scar!

ABOUT ME: I'm just a regular mark that likes to show up after a burn, sore, or tear in the skin. I'm extremely loyal and will stick with you through thick and thin.

LOOKING FOR: A body to commit to for months, years, or even a lifetime if the situation is right.

TALENTS: Helping to repair your skin after an injury. I'm also a great conversation starter.

Scab! (BUT MY FRIENDS CALL ME "PATCH")

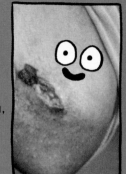

ABOUT ME: I come from a very tight-knit family of bloody platelets. Whenever Scrape or Cut appears, we rush to the scene and band together to act like glue, forming a protective bandage keeping your insides in, where they belong.

APPEARANCE: If you see me in the wild, you'll know me by my crusty, irregular, reddish brown looks. And please don't judge me by my rough exterior. There's a lot of good happening underneath.

FAVORITE QUOTE: "Pick Me! Pick Me!"

Bruise! (AKA BRUISER, THE BRUISEMEISTER, BRUIZOODLE, BRUIZEEZY, AND BRUCE)

LIKES: Trauma and drama!

WOULDN'T BE HERE WITHOUT: All the tiny blood vessels (capillaries) that burst before me. Because of them, I have all of these amazing colors.

SOMETIMES I FEEL: TRAPPED . . . under the skin.

WHAT I WANT PEOPLE TO KNOW ABOUT ME:
I DON'T NEED A BAND-AID!

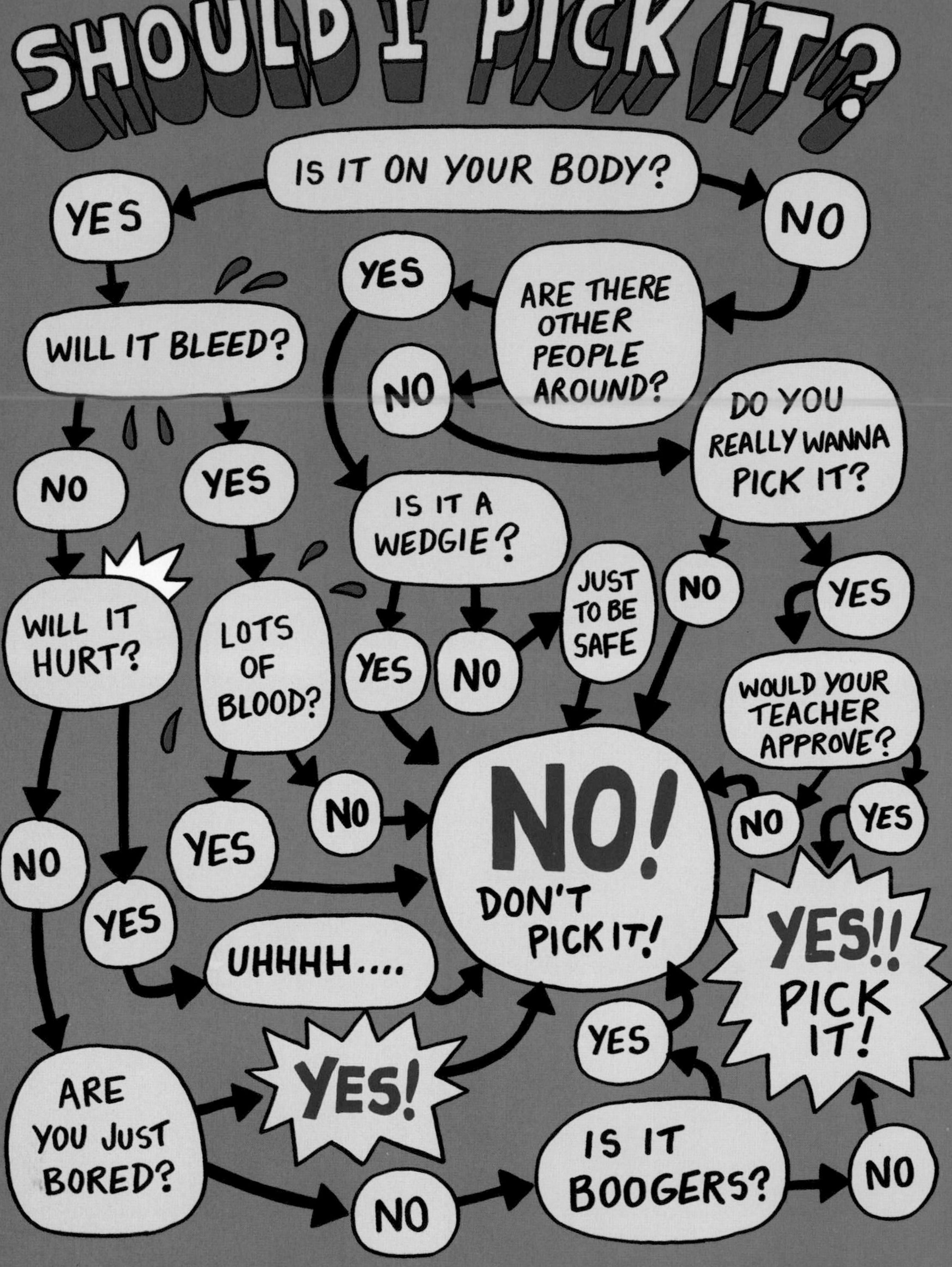
SHOULD I PICK IT?
IS IT ON YOUR BODY?
YES
NO
WILL IT BLEED?
YES
ARE THERE OTHER PEOPLE AROUND?
NO
DO YOU REALLY WANNA PICK IT?
NO
YES
IS IT A WEDGIE?
JUST TO BE SAFE
NO
YES
WILL IT HURT?
LOTS OF BLOOD?
YES
NO
WOULD YOUR TEACHER APPROVE?
NO
YES
NO
YES
NO! DON'T PICK IT!
NO
YES
YES!! PICK IT!
UHHHH....
YES
YES!
ARE YOU JUST BORED?
IS IT BOOGERS?
NO
NO

SWEAT

SWEAT IS COOL!

Eww! What's That Smell?

Oh, you think that smell is bad? Well then, saddle up while we tell you what's *causing* it! See, one might be inclined to blame it on sweat. But, fun fact: Sweat is actually odorless to us humans, meaning that we really can't smell it *at all*. In fact, that meaty odor wafting from your pits is thanks in part to a certain group of microbes. These hungry microbes chow down on little bits of sweat molecules, leaving behind even smaller bits that can really cause a stink.

YUM!

Um . . . I wasn't talking about me. I'm a kid. My armpits smell fine. I was talking about my teenage brother.

Sure, your armpits might smell fine *for now*. The reason your kid armpits don't stink is simply because your body doesn't make enough of the kind of sweat that turns into BO, or body odor . . . *yet*. Teenagers, on the other hand, are busy churning out a whole new kind of armpit sweat called apocrine sweat. And they make *a lot* of it. It's a thick and oily all-you-can-eat buffet for hungry microbes looking for a snack. They eat, and eat, and eat, leaving little bits of stinktastic sweat molecules behind!

THERE'S A FEAST HERE!

So kids don't stink at all? Can you tell that to my grandma?

Not so fast. While your armpits might not smell like cheese-smothered corn chips on a hot summer day, your body can produce another kind of sweat that does stink.

HOW MANY SWEATS ARE THERE?!

We'll get to that in a minute. Humans of *all* ages produce a kind of sweat called eccrine sweat. The purpose of eccrine sweat is to help control your body temperature, especially as it starts to heat up. This sweat is thin and watery, and can sometimes cause your clothes to smell musty or mildewy.

Gross.

Yep. But it's also one of the many tricks our body has to keep us alive and healthy.

Healthy and GROSS.

Healthy and gross.

Anything for Science!
To collect sweat, some researchers have been known to have their test subjects exercise in giant plastic bags!

Gimme the Sweats!

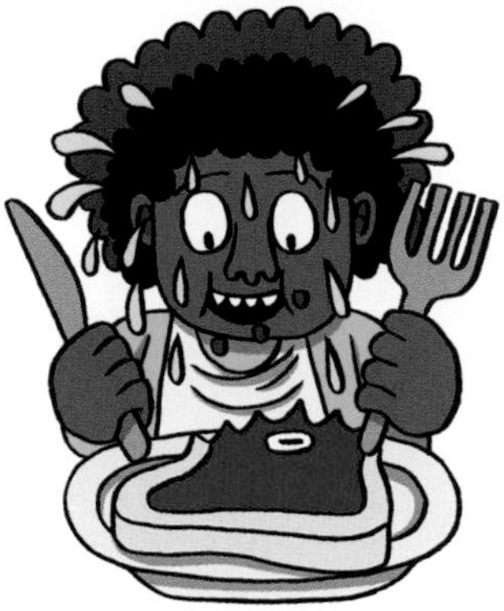

Meat Sweats The phenomenon of intense sweating that can occur after eating an excessively meaty meal.

★ While not an actual medical term, there is some science to back up the ol' meat sweats. See, meat, especially red meat, requires a lot of energy and heat from our body to digest or break down. It's this combination of energy and heat that causes the body to sweat.

★ Where you can find meat sweats in the wild: competitive hot-dog-eating contests.

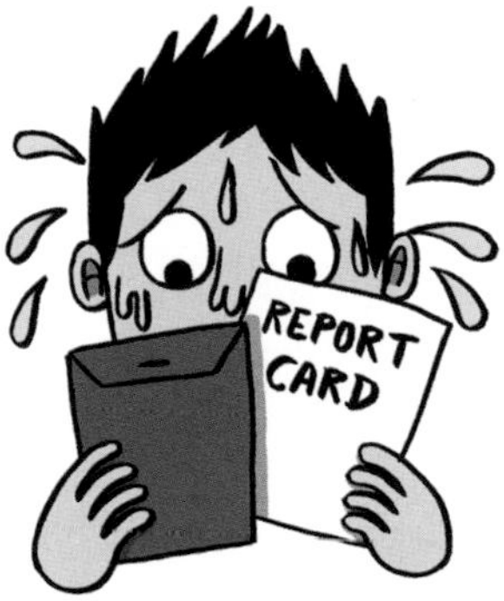
REPORT CARD

Flop Sweats The sudden and spontaneous heavy sweating that occurs during a moment of extreme nervousness, especially when a person is experiencing a fear of failure.

★ Where you can find flop sweats in the wild: piano recitals, school plays, report card day.

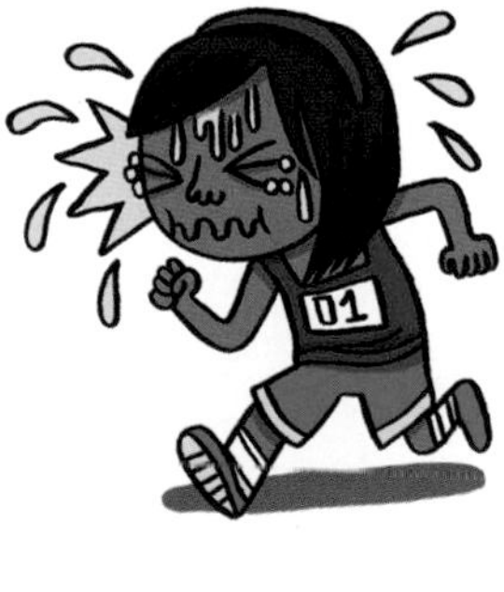
01

Cake Sweats These are the super-salty sweats that can sting your eyeballs while you're running around. Cake sweats usually happen when you're putting more water than salt into your body. Some people have saltier sweat than others. How salty are YOUR sweats?

NAILS

Nailed It!

THEN → NOW

On the tip of each finger and toe, there is a little protective plate known as a nail. While we still don't know for sure why we have them, some scientists believe that they have evolved in humans from claws of our ancient ancestors. Both fingernails and toenails are made of a hard, flexible substance called keratin, the same substance that helps to make up our hair, the top layer of our skin, and even the hooves on a horse.

NAILS GROW A TENTH OF A MILLIMETER PER DAY.

KIDS' FINGERNAILS GROW TWICE AS FAST AS THOSE OF TEENS AND ADULTS. IF YOU DON'T BELIEVE US, TRY CHALLENGING YOUR FAMILY IN A WEEK-LONG RACE AND SEE FOR YOURSELF!

NAILS GROW FASTER DURING THE DAY AND IN THE SUMMER.

RIGHT-HANDED? LEFT-HANDED? FINGERNAILS GROW FASTEST ON YOUR DOMINANT HAND.

NAILS ARE AS STRONG AS HORSE HOOVES.

RECORD-BREAKING WOW!

Shridhar Chillal, of Pune, India, spent 66 years NOT trimming his fingernails. But in 2018, at the age of 82, he decided it was time. One by one, he clipped his nails that, combined, measured in at a length of 29 feet, 10.1 inches (909.6cm). That's almost half the length of a bowling alley! But that's not all! Chillal is now the proud Guiness World Record Holder for Longest Fingernails on a Single Hand!

SHOULD I BITE 'EM?

WOW!

IF YOU LOSE A FINGERNAIL, IT COULD TAKE THREE TO SIX MONTHS TO GROW IT BACK.

ABOUT HALF OF KIDS AND TEENS BITE THEIR NAILS.

FINGERNAILS HELP TO DISTINGUISH PRIMATES LIKE US FROM OTHER MAMMALS WITH CLAWS.

YOUR THUMBNAIL GROWS THE SLOWEST OF ALL YOUR FINGER-NAILS.

FINGERNAILS GROW ABOUT THREE TIMES FASTER THAN TOENAILS.

HAIR

The Long and Short of It

While most other warm-blooded land animals have fur to help keep them warm, we humans are left to fend for ourselves. Our bodies are almost entirely covered in hair, but for the most part, it's very fine: more of a fuzz than a fur. Our bare skin is pretty good when it comes to keeping our bodies cool, but in colder climates, we depend on thick clothing to keep us warm and toasty.

Hair Today, Gone Tomorrow

On average, humans have over 100,000 hairs warming our big ol' heads. If you don't believe us, try counting! Each strand grows continuously for anywhere from two to six years. After that, these hairs take a little break and eventually fall out on their own. About 100 hairs every day! Why don't we notice these hairs falling out? They're constantly being replaced by brand-new hairs sprouting from the very same follicles. Just think of your head as a bustling hairport of arrivals and departures!

THE FOLLICLE FACTORY

WELCOME TO THE FOLLICLE FACTORY, WHERE WE GROW HAIR BECAUSE WE CARE!

AT THE FOLLICLE FACTORY, EACH HAIR IS ASSIGNED AND GROWN FROM ITS OWN DEEP, NARROW SHAFT KNOWN AS — YOU GUESSED IT— A FOLLICLE.

WE'VE GOT FOLLICLES BIG AND FOLLICLES SMALL. CHOOSE A SPECIFIC SHAPE AND SIZE, OR BRACE YOURSELF FOR A MAJOR SURPRISE.

FOLLICLE SHAPES

ROUND FOLLICLE SEMI-OVAL FOLLICLE FLAT-OVAL FOLLICLE

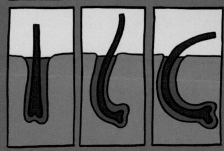

LET'S HEAR WHAT SOME OF OUR SATISFIED CUSTOMERS HAVE TO SAY!

I WENT WITH A PACK OF ROUND FOLLICLES BECAUSE IT WAS ON SALE, AND NOW MY HEAD LOOKS LIKE IT'S COVERED IN STRAIGHT BLADES OF GRASS!

FOR FABULOUS COILS AND CURLS, I HIGHLY RECOMMEND A FLAT-OVAL FOLLICLE!

GO FOR THE SEMI-OVAL FOLLICLE! WAVY HAIR DON'T CARE!

CUSTOMERS CAN EXPECT TO LOSE ABOUT ONE HUNDRED HEAD HAIRS EVERY SINGLE DAY, BUT REPLACEMENT HAIRS ARE FREE!

Two Types of Hair

Have you ever wondered why the hair on your arms, knuckles, and earlobes doesn't grow as long as the hairs on your head? Well, that's because they're a completely different type of hair. In fact, there are two main types of hair on the human body: vellus hair and terminal hair.

Vellus hair (AKA peach fuzz) is the soft, fine hair that covers most of the body, especially in females and kids. This hair is so light it's almost translucent and difficult to see from far away. Vellus hair makes itself known when it stands at attention during a moment of goose bumps.

Peach Fuzz

Terminal hair is thicker than vellus hair and can be found growing out of the top of your head. It adds a little warmth and acts as your head's personal shield from the sun. Teenagers and grownups (especially men) might also find terminal hair covering their arms, legs, armpits, and beyond.

Terminal Hair

Where you WON'T find hair

These are all examples of **glabrous skin:** free from hair follicles, but heavy on padding.

The palms of your hands

Your lips

The soles of your feet

EVEN A WEREWOLF DOESN'T GET HAIR HERE!

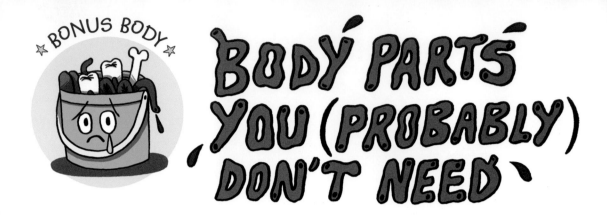

BODY PARTS YOU (PROBABLY) DON'T NEED

By now, you've likely realized that your body is a truly wow piece of human machinery. A soft, squishy, and sometimes slimy factory of intricate parts all working together to keep you alive and help you thrive. But have you ever wondered about the parts of your body that don't do . . . anything? Let's explore the most (seemingly) useless parts of the human body!

THE APPENDIX

We see you, appendix, you thin little four-inch (10-cm) tube that hangs out there in the lower right area of the abdomen. To this day, scientists aren't sure what you do. There is a theory that you serve as a little hangout for certain kinds of "good" bacteria and therefore help to keep infections away. But we still don't know for sure. So in the meantime, appendix, you don't bother us, and we won't bother you. Deal?

Appendix

THE TAILBONE

Tailbone

Oh, tailbone. There you sit, at the end of the spine, right where a tail would be. But are you an actual tail? Nope! You're a little bony nub left over from the days when our ancestors had tails. Having an actual tail would be pretty *wow,* but it would also make it challenging to wear pants.

76

GOOD NEWS! I'VE DECIDED TO GET A TAIL!

I'M NOT SURE THAT'S A THING YOU CAN DO.

SURE I CAN! OUR ANCESTORS HAD TAILS, WHY CAN'T I?

WELL, FOR ONE, ONCE WE HUMANS EVOLVED TO WALK ON TWO FEET, WE STOPPED NEEDING TAILS FOR BALANCE.

OH YEAH, I DON'T NEED IT FOR BALANCE, JUST FOR DECORATION.

ALSO OUR ANCESTORS DIDN'T WEAR PANTS.

ON SECOND THOUGHT, MAYBE I CAN LIVE WITHOUT A TAIL.

WISDOM TEETH

Dear wisdom teeth, we're sorry, but you gotta go. Sure, you were there for our early ancestors as they munched on leaves, roots, and raw meats. But times have changed. We eat soft things now. Like ice cream and marshmallows and hot dog buns right out of the bag. No hard feelings, but it's time for us to part ways. Thank you for your service, wisdom teeth, but your job here is done.

TONSILS

Tonsils

THINGS YOUR WISDOM TEETH WILL NOT DO FOR YOU:

- GIVE YOU A "SMART MOUTH"
- HELP YOU WITH SCHOOL
- MAKE YOU GOOD AT STANDARDIZED TESTS
- HOLD THE SECRETS TO ENLIGHTENMENT
- TELL YOU RIGHT FROM WRONG; YOU'RE ON YOUR OWN, PAL!

Sweet tonsils, you've always been there for me: stepping in to stop bacteria from getting past my throat and stepping up as a real team player of my immune system. But you keep getting infected. And when you get infected, I get sick. And when I get sick, I get ice cream. And I love ice cream! But ice cream is less fun to eat when it has a job to do, like soothing my swollen sore throat. Tonsils, if this keeps up, we're going to have to part ways. And by "part ways" I mean I'm going to have to have you removed from my throat.

HOW WE MOVE

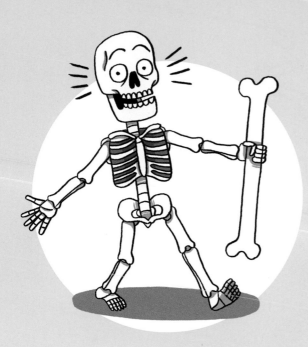

Bones
There Is a Skeleton Living Inside You!

Muscles
Turning Your Body into a Tyrannosaurus FLEX!

BONES

There Is a Skeleton Living Inside You!

Um . . . not to freak you out or anything, but, uh . . . THERE IS AN ACTUAL SKELETON HIDING INSIDE YOUR BODY!

MINDY & GUY

AHHHHHHHHHH!!!

YOU

Calm down! You need this thing! It gives your body shape and structure while protecting all your internal organs and bodily systems. Without it, you'd just be one big floppy mess of skin and guts.

MINDY & GUY

Exhale. Good point.

YOU

These bones are also alive.

MINDY & GUY

AHHHHHHHHHHHHHHHHHH! A LIVING SKELETON? IN MY BODY?!

YOU

Yep! Alive, growing, and changing just like the rest of your body. If your bones weren't alive and growing, you'd still look like a baby.

MINDY & GUY

Why are you doing this to me?!

YOU

Speaking of babies, did you know that on the day you were born, you had 300 bones? And by the time you're a grownup, you'll have only 206.

MINDY & GUY

WHAT?! WHY ARE MY BONES DISAPPEARING?!

YOU

Well, they're not exactly disappearing. Some of your bones are actually fusing, or growing together.

MINDY & GUY

And . . . that's a good thing?

YOU

It's a natural thing. It happens to all of us as we grow.

MINDY & GUY

Sigh. I'd really like to meet this skeleton someday.

YOU

You're going to be waiting a long time.

MINDY & GUY

The Bone Hall of Strain

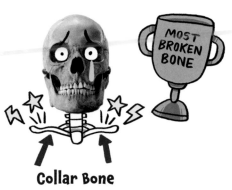

While bones have the strength to carry a heavy load throughout your lifetime, they are occasionally known to break when put under more pressure than they can handle. This can happen suddenly (falling out of a tree) or over a period of time (climbing too many trees).

MOST FRAGILE

 Winner: The number-one most commonly broken bone in the human body is the clavicle, or collarbone. And you have two of them connecting your shoulder blades to your sternum, or breastbone. The clavicle is also the only bone in the body to lie horizontally.

Collar Bone

 First runner up: the lacrimal bone. While not commonly broken, the lacrimal bone is in the running for the most fragile bone in the human body. And you have two of them: one in the middle of each eye socket.

Lacrimal Bone

1ST RUNNER UP

 Second runner up: the stapes. The stapes is the tiny stirrup-shaped bone in the middle ear, and while it's super fragile, it's also hard to find from the outside. So if you somehow manage to break a stapes, you'll have some explaining to do.

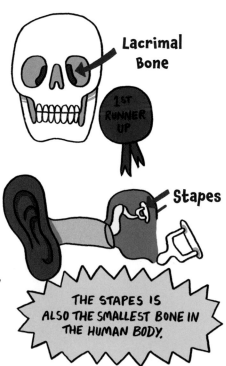

Stapes

THE STAPES IS ALSO THE SMALLEST BONE IN THE HUMAN BODY.

STRONGEST BONE

★ **The award for Strongest Bone in the Human Body goes to . . .** the femur! The femur, also the longest bone in your body, is located in your thigh, and it's pretty hard to break. So don't even try, okay?

CASTS

They're Not Just for Collecting Autographs and Attention

Casts and splints actually help to hold our broken bones still, so they can repair themselves correctly. This requires time and patience, but the results are always worth it.

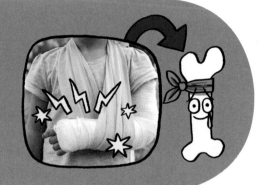

Fact Snacks

BONES: THEY TAKE A LICKIN' AND KEEP ON KICKIN'!

★ Every bone in your body is connected to another bone, EXCEPT for the hyoid, a horseshoe-shaped bone found in your throat.

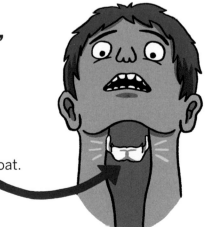

★ Some of your bones are able to absorb up to two to three times your body weight in force!

★ One in every two hundred people are born with an extra rib! Most people have twenty-four ribs, twelve on each side.

wow!

★ More than half the bones in your body are found in your hands and feet (106 out of 206)!

How to Care for Your Skeleton

The bones that make up your skeleton are designed to last a lifetime, but over time, they start to lose strength. Here are some ways to support your skeleton so it can continue to support you:

Feed your skeleton: It might look bony, but you can help keep your skeleton strong by feeding it foods rich in calcium and vitamin D. Skeletons love foods like broccoli, kale, salmon, tuna, cheese, yogurt, eggs, and almond butter.

Walk your skeleton: Skeletons need exercise. Aim for one hour of weight-bearing exercise a day. These can include walking, running, jumping, or climbing. These kinds of exercises work with your muscles and gravity to put pressure on your bones, and that pressure strengthens them and helps them grow.

Talk to your skeleton: Though not scientifically proven to help, waking up in the morning and thanking your skeleton for all of its LITERAL SUPPORT can't hurt either. Thanks, Skelly!

Battle of the Broken Bones

While breaking a bone can be extremely painful, the good news is that our bones have the ability to regrow and repair themselves.

MUSCLES

Turning Your Body into a Tyrannosaurus FLEX!

When we think of muscles, we often picture Olympic athletes, professional dancers, and superhero grandmas picking up whole school buses full of kindergarteners and moving them out of harm's way. But did you know that you, too, have some pretty powerful muscles? In fact, every single movement in your body is made by your muscular system and controlled by your brain. From the teeny-tiny stapedius muscle in your ear to the gigantic gluteus maximus in your butt, your muscles are responsible for keeping your body moving and upright.

Muscle Matter

Muscle is made of long cells called fibers. Using the body's energy, muscles can pull the parts of your body in different directions by contracting, or shortening. This is what happens when you get out of bed in the morning or brush your teeth, but it also happens in ways you don't even think about—like when you blink or your heart beats.

Let's meet the three different types of muscles in your body.

Skeletal muscle:

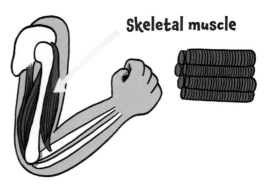

Skeletal muscle

I pretty much hang out in places like your arms and legs. Your bone and skin would say that I'm clingy. Because I *am!* In fact, your bones wouldn't even be able to move without me! Shrink, shorten—I do whatever it takes to move your bones from one place to the next. But I can't do it entirely on my own. I'm a voluntary muscle, which means I need to be told what to do by *you*. Like a genie in a bottle, your wish is my command.

Smooth muscle:

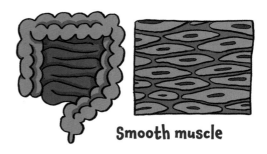

Smooth muscle

Unlike skeletal muscle, I tend to work behind the scenes. I'm packed together in flat layered sheets, and I line the walls of your digestive system, help to open up your airways, and control your bladder. (You're welcome!) I'm a smooth operator, working automatically 24/7, and don't wait to be told what to do. In fact, I'm going to work for you whether you want me to or not. Why? Because it is my job to keep your body functioning properly, and I will continue to do my best to never let you down.

Cardiac muscle:

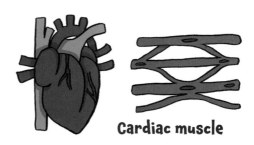

Cardiac muscle

At the heart of it, I'm a bit of a life-or-death situation. In fact, I form the walls of your heart. Unlike these other muscles, I never, ever get tired. I just expand and contract all day every day to keep your heart beating to the rhythm of your life.

What in the Wow?

★ The word "muscle" comes from the Latin word for "mouse." Ancient Romans thought that muscles moving under the skin looked like mice running around.

★ A grownup's body weight is between 30 percent and 40 percent muscle.

★ You have more than six hundred skeletal muscles in your body.

★ Your eye muscles move more than one hundred thousand times a day.

★ Every single one of the five million hairs on your body has its own muscle.

★ There are three times as many skeletal muscles in your body as there are bones.

WELCOME TO MUSCLE MANIA: A SHOWCASE OF THE MUSCLES WITH THE MOST.

TODAY WE'LL BE HONORING THE STRONGEST, LONGEST, LARGEST, AND SMALLEST MUSCLES IN THE HUMAN BODY!

AND HERE COMES OUR FIRST HONOREE. KNOWN FOR PULLING WITH MORE FORCE THAN VIRTUALLY ANY OTHER MUSCLE IN THE BODY, IT'S ARGUABLY THE STRONGEST OF THEM ALL. GIVE IT UP FOR THE LOWER LEG'S OWN **SOLEUS**!

NEXT UP, IT'S THE LONG AND LEAN SKELETAL MUSCLE RUNNING THE LENGTH OF YOUR THIGH. PUT YOUR HANDS TOGETHER FOR THE LONGEST MUSCLE IN THE HUMAN BODY, **SARTORIUS**!

MAKE NO BUTTS ABOUT IT, PEOPLE, THE BIGGEST MUSCLE IN THE BODY IS FOUND IN THE BOOTY! IT'S FUN TO LAUGH ABOUT, AND IT HELPS YOU TO STAND UP WHEN YOU'RE SITTING DOWN. IT'S THE **GLUTEUS MAXIMUS**!

AND WE CAN'T HONOR THE BIGGEST WITHOUT PAYING TRIBUTE TO THE SMALLEST. ALLOW US TO INTRODUCE YOU TO THE SMALLEST MUSCLE IN YOUR HUMAN BODY. IT'S LOCATED IN YOUR EAR AND IS ONLY 0.04 INCHES (1 MM) LONG. LET'S GIVE A BIG ROUND OF APPLAUSE FOR THE **STAPEDIUS**!

AAAAAHHH! IT'S SO TINY!

THAT'S ALL FOR TONIGHT, WOWZERS. THANK YOU FOR JOINING US THIS WEEK FOR MUSCLE MANIA!

BONUS BODY

THE ARMPITS

The pits? They have names! Axilla is the anatomical name for armpit. Wow your doctor and confuse your friends by referring to your armpits as your axillae.

Are You Sick? Ask Your Armpits!

While your armpits can't speak (if they do, you should consult your doctor), they *can* tell you how well you're doing. Each armpit contains a bunch of little lymph nodes. Lymph nodes are like teeny-tiny beanbags sitting under the surface of your skin, and their job is to filter out and fight off bad germs that can make you sick. Most of the time you can't see or feel them. But if you *do* feel them, it's most likely because they're swollen. And swollen lymph nodes could be your armpits' way of telling you, "You've got an infection!"

Your armpit is one of the warmest parts of your body. If you don't believe us, tuck a couple slices of bread in there and see how long it takes to heat them up. Your own personal bread warmers!

Things you can do with your armpits:

★ Pop a water balloon

★ Warm up a doughnut

★ Stink out an elevator

★ Hold a paperback book

★ Reveal a secret message (HI!)

★ Hide a walnut

Things you cannot do with your armpits:

★ Tickle yourself

Why Can't You Tickle Yourself?

Have you ever attempted to tickle yourself? Didn't work, did it? Scientists at the University of Cambridge think it may have to do with your cerebellum, the part of your brain that anticipates what different things feel like. When you tickle yourself, your cerebellum knows what to expect and isn't impressed. But when someone else tickles you? WHERE DID THAT COME FROM?! In short, some scientists believe that the reason it's impossible to tickle yourself is because YOU CAN'T SURPRISE YOURSELF!

PUMP IT UP, GO WITH THE FLOW

Heart
It Lubs You!

Blood
Not as Gross When It's Inside Your Body

Lungs
[More Than] Just a Couple of Ol' Windbags

Urinary System
Pee-Pee Power!

HEART

It Lubs You!

If your brain is the master control center of your body, then your heart (located in the center of your chest) is the engine that powers it. Working tirelessly from the time before you were even born, this unique and powerful muscle will continue to beat for you each and every moment of your life without taking any breaks. In fact, the heart will beat 2.5 *billion* times in the average lifetime. That's one hundred thousand beats per day!

Wow Don't You . . . Gimme a Beat!

How to calculate your resting heart rate in BPM (beats per minute): Gently press the index and middle fingers of one hand on the opposite wrist, just below the base of your thumb. When you feel the beat, count the number of pulses you feel in fifteen seconds and multiply that number by four. Your answer will be your BPM, or beats per minute!

Newborn babies 120 to 160 bpm

Kids 70 to 120 bpm

Well-trained athletes 40 to 160 bpm

Adults 60 to 100 bpm

BUT WHAT EXACTLY HAPPENS EVERY TIME YOUR HEART DROPS A BEAT?

BLOOD, GUY RAZ.

BLOOD?

WITH EVERY BEAT, YOUR HEART IS PUMPING BLOOD AND DELIVERING IT TO THE REST OF YOUR BODY USING A COMPLEX HIGHWAY SYSTEM OF VESSELS KNOWN AS ARTERIES, VEINS, AND CAPILLARIES.

BLOOD ALL AROUND! BLOOD FOR EVERYONE! CARE FOR SOME FREE BLOOD?

AH . . . AND IN THAT BLOOD THERE'S OXYGEN, CARBON DIOXIDE, NUTRIENTS, AND EVEN HEAT, RIGHT?

EXACTORITOS! THEY ALL HITCH A RIDE ON THE OL' BLOODMOBILE.

GOOD MORNING, MUSCLES! SPECIAL DELIVERY!

95

Lub-DUB: What's That Sound?

Close your eyes and think of your heart as a little
apple-shaped whoopie cushion filled with blood.
On that whoopie cushion are four little flappy trapdoors
called valves. These doors open and close to allow the
blood to travel into your body, making that famous "lub-DUB" sound that can be
heard through a doctor's stethoscope. So the next time you get the chance to
hear that sound up close, picture your heart beating just for you! Awwww.

Fact Snacks

★ A newborn baby's heart is about the size of a Ping-Pong ball. A kid's heart is the size of their fist, just about. A grownup's heart is usually bigger than their fist, but everyone is different.

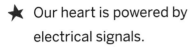

★ Our heart is powered by electrical signals.

★ The average adult man's heart weighs about twelve ounces (340 g)—that's as heavy as a can of soup!

★ In 2017, researchers from Colorado University found that when two people in love hold hands, their hearts start to beat in sync!

★ Your heart makes enough energy each day to power a truck for twenty miles (32 km)!

★ On average, your heart beats one hundred thousand times a day, pumping two thousand gallons (7,570 L) of blood through your body!

GET PUMPED!

BLOOD

Not as Gross When It's Inside Your Body

Blood is a bustling delivery system working hard to keep you healthy and alive. It does this by moving oxygen, fuel, and germ-fighting cells throughout your body while helping to get rid of the junk in there you don't need. And just like your blood-pumping heart, it's working constantly, around the clock, and without fail. That's a busy bloodmobile!

OKAY, BLOOD CELLS! LET'S GET TO WORK! I NEED YOU TO DELIVER SOME OF THIS CARBON DIOXIDE TO THE LUNGS, AND THEN DROP THIS POOL OF WATER OFF AT THE KIDNEYS.

AND WHILE YOU'RE AT IT, SEE IF YOU CAN GO FIGHT OFF THAT PESKY INFECTION THAT'S INVADING THE BLADDER.

Do You Know What's in YOUR Blood? Get to Know Your Cells and Platelets!

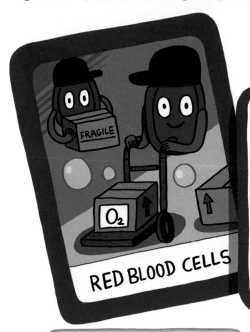

RED BLOOD CELLS

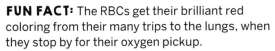

TEAM: The Notorious RBCs, AKA the Red Blood Cells

KNOWN FOR: Delivering oxygen to cells and removing carbon dioxide

FUN FACT: The RBCs get their brilliant red coloring from their many trips to the lungs, when they stop by for their oxygen pickup.

LIFE EXPECTANCY: Four months

WHAT?! Only four months?!

It's fine! Your bones are making RBCs every day to replace the dead ones. RIP, old RBCs.

Wow, those WBCs have a tough job!

TEAM: The WBC Fighters, AKA the White Blood Cells

KNOWN FOR: Fighting infections and defending the body against germy invaders like bad bacteria and viruses

FUN FACT: While there are way less WBCs in your blood than RBCs, when you get sick, your body can just make more. A whole army of little fighters battle to keep you healthy when germs threaten to make you sick.

LIFE EXPECTANCY: A few hours to a few years

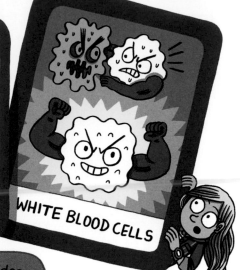

WHITE BLOOD CELLS

Yeah, don't get too attached. Besides, new WBCs are being made every day.

TEAM: The Clots, AKA the Platelets

KNOWN FOR: Teaming up, first-responder style, to seal off the leak when a blood vessel breaks. Controlling the blood and keeping it from going bonkerballs both inside and outside your body.

LIFE EXPECTANCY: Ten days

PLATELETS

But let me guess, more platelets are created every day.

You know it! Right there in the ol' bones.

Fact Snacks

★ Your body holds about a gallon and a half (5.7 L) of blood.

★ A newborn baby's body holds only one cup of blood.

★ The smallest blood vessel in your body is three times smaller than the width of a human hair.

★ The blood in your body travels 11,800 miles (19,000 km) a day. That's about *four times* the distance it would take to fly between New York and Los Angeles!

★ Your blood makes up almost 8 percent of your total body weight.

★ One blood cell goes through the heart and around the body one thousand times a day.

★ Your body makes two million new red blood cells every second to replace the ones that die.

DON'T TRY THIS AT HOME EXPERIMENT

OW!

Blood Around the World

Did you know that if you were to lay out a grownup's blood vessels in a line, they would stretch over one hundred thousand miles (161,000 km)? That's enough to circle Earth nearly four times!

The Circulatory System Cycle

Okay, here's the game plan: Heart! Listen up! With every beat, you are going to pump blood throughout the body!

Arteries usually look red and carry blood away from the heart.

Blood! Once you're released from the heart, you'll need to quickly deliver oxygen to every cell in the body! And no cutting corners! I don't want to see any hands or feet falling asleep, you hear?

Actually, that's a common misconception . . . limbs fall asleep because of nerve pressure, not lack of blood.

And ANOTHER thing: when you finish the job, head on back to the heart.

Veins usually look blue and carry blood back to the heart.

Lungs! Once the blood is back to the heart, I'm sending it over to you to pick up some more oxygen so we can repeat this cycle again and again for the rest of this person's life! Got it? Good! Now let's get to work!

Veins appear blue

Arteries appear red

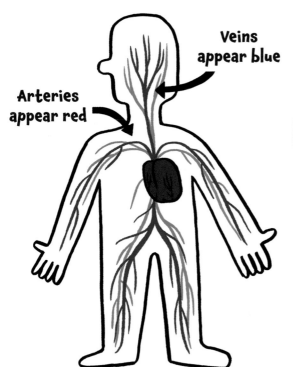

LUNGS

[More Than] Just a Couple of Ol' Windbags

Inside your chest, there are two large bags known as lungs. And to put it mildly, they're kind of a big deal. Without lungs, you wouldn't be able to breathe, talk, cry, scream, sing, or even hiccup! Every second of every day, your lungs are swapping gases to help you live. Lungs help you to breathe in vital oxygen that enters the bloodstream while getting rid of the carbon dioxide that your body doesn't need. In fact, this cycle is so important, your lungs actually have their own rib cage of bones just to protect them. A built-in suit of armor custom-made for a couple of supreme windbags.

Feel the Lung Power

Put one hand on your chest and take a deep breath. Notice how your chest expands and gets bigger? Now, release that breath and watch as your chest returns to its normal size. That's LUNG POWER, baby!

Mindy Interviews Her Lungs

MINDY: So, Lungs, what would you say is your purpose in life?

LUNGS: Well, we'd have to say we're dedicated to helping bring oxygen into your body while getting waste gases out of your bloodstream.

MINDY: Cool. Thanks. But . . . um . . . do you always talk in unison?

LUNGS: We do everything in unison.

MINDY: So are you twins?

RIGHT LUNG: Not exactly. Left Lung over here is actually smaller than I am.

LEFT LUNG: BECAUSE I HAVE TO SHARE A ROOM WITH YOUR HEART!

MINDY: Got it! Got it. Left Lung, you share some of my chest with my heart, so you're a little smaller. No big deal.

LEFT LUNG: Let's just leave size out of it.

MINDY: Okay, so how would you describe yourself to someone who has never met you in person?

RIGHT LUNG: Well, on the outside, we're pink, squishy, and spongy.

LEFT LUNG: But on the inside we look like pink broccoli.

MINDY: WHAT?!

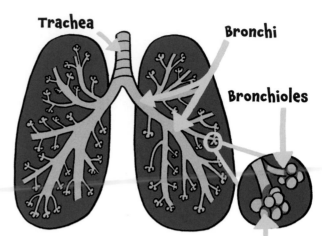

Trachea

Bronchi

Bronchioles

Alveoli

RIGHT LUNG: See, we are full of all of these little broccoli-like trees called bronchioles. And each bronchiole stems from a larger bronchus that splits off from your trachea.

MINDY: Oh yeah, the trachea is that windpipe tube that carries air between my throat and lungs, right?

RIGHT LUNG: Right. So when you breathe, the oxygen comes into your trachea, then branches out into each bronchus and works its way through all of those little bronchiole stems until they reach the alveoli.

MINDY: You mean ravioli?

LEFT LUNG: NO.

RIGHT LUNG: See, at the ends of each bronchiole stem, there are bunches of teeny-tiny airbags called alveoli (al-VEE-uh-lie), and they're covered in a web of super-thin blood vessels called capillaries.

LEFT LUNG: And every time you breathe in or inhale, these six hundred million alveoli fill up with air, and your lungs get bigger!

RIGHT LUNG: And it's because of these alveoli that the oxygen from the air is able to make it into your blood, through your heart, and back out to the rest of your body.

MINDY: Wow! Thanks, alveoli! But what happens when I breathe out or exhale?

LEFT LUNG: Well, the same thing happens, only in reverse!

RIGHT LUNG: And when you breathe out, carbon dioxide leaves the blood, passes through the capillaries and the alveoli and into the trachea, ready to be breathed out!

MINDY: Swappin' gases and taking names!

LUNGS: That's us!

Lungs by the Numbers

★ 18 to 30: The number of breaths an average six- to twelve-year-old takes in a minute.

★ More than 2,000 gallons (7,570 L): The amount of air a typical adult breathes in and out in one day.

★ 1,500 miles (2,400 km): The total length of all the lungs' airways (bronchi and bronchioles) strung end to end.

★ 600 million: The number of combined alveoli in your two lungs. That's more than enough to cover a tennis court! DO NOT TRY THIS.

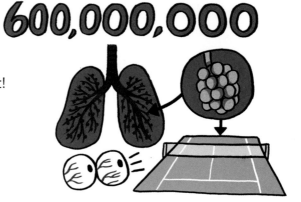

★ Over 500 million: The number of breaths a person who lives to age eighty will take in their lifetime.

URINARY SYSTEM

Pee-Pee Power!

Pee, AKA urine, is more than just a bathroom word and your body's way of interrupting you during a movie. It's also your body's way of taking out the trash. In fact, pee is how we get rid of extra water that we don't need, extra nutrients that we can't absorb, and waste that we don't want. Consider your urinary system part of your body's janitorial staff and celebrate it once in a while. (Did somebody say pee party?!)

Our urinary system is made up of four main parts. Let's meet them!

Kidneys: "We grab waste from your blood and make pee."

Ureters: "We're pee-pee pathways! Just a couple of tubes connecting your kidneys to your bladder."

Bladder: "I'm a big sack of pee!"

Urethra: "Last train to Pee Town. Next stop: Toiletsville!"

Kidneys

Bladder

Ureters

Urethra

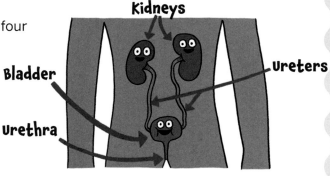

What is that Urethra talking about?!

It's Urethra's way of saying that it's the tube you pee out of.

Ohhh . . .

Kidneys (NOT to Be Confused with "Kid Knees")

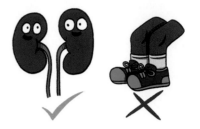

During digestion, your body takes out a bunch of good nutrients from the foods you eat, and in that process, it also creates some waste. And that's where your kidneys kick in. They grab all the waste and extra nutrients your body can't absorb and turn some of it into pee. It's your body's way of taking out the trash.

Can't find your kidneys? That's probably a good sign that they're right where they're supposed to be—inside your body. In fact, they're located on your back, behind your rib cage. To find your kidneys, put your hands on your hips and move them up until you find your ribs. Now notice where your thumbs land. That's generally the spot where your kidneys live.

Your kidneys are shaped like, well . . . giant kidney beans! Each of your two kidneys is about five inches (13 cm) long and three inches (8 cm) wide, or about the same size as an adult fist. You need at least one kidney to live, but you have two just in case. The job of a kidney is so important our bodies come with a backup!

Your kidneys are a good example of something called "bilateral symmetry." Our bodies often grow doubles of certain parts, with one almost identical copy appearing on either side of our body: two eyes, two ears, two arms, two legs, and two kidneys. The left and right sides of our bodies look like mirror images of each other. Imagine if the same were true for the top and bottom halves. Two heads? Two bellies? Two BUTTS?!

The Bladder

The bladder acts as a little grapefruit-size sack or pouch for your pee. It holds roughly one and a half to two cups (350–475 mL) of liquid, and once it gets to be about half full, it *lets you know*.

Asparagus Whiz

In 1791, Benjamin Franklin proved himself to be a real asparagus whiz when he wrote the words, "A few stems of asparagus eaten, shall give our urine a disagreeable odor." *What?* While he might not have been the first human to smell their own pee after eating asparagus, he was the first to *write about it* in a very public and poetic way. Way to take the pee out of the potty, Ben Franklin!

So what makes our pee stink after eating asparagus? While scientists don't know for sure what causes our pee to smell like asparagus, there is a widely agreed-upon hypothesis (or educated guess) that the stink is created as the asparagus is broken down in the digestion process.

In 2016, a team of scientists from Harvard University got almost seven thousand willing participants to eat a bunch of asparagus and then SMELL THEIR OWN PEE! What they discovered was that only 40 percent could detect the stink! As it turns out, the ability to smell this particular odor *may* be linked to genetics, meaning that it's something passed down from one generation to the next. Do we smell a family science experiment coming on?

> Stinky pee? NOT ME!

> Not so fast! EVERYONE'S pee smells like asparagus after eating it. BUT (and this is a BIG BUTT) not everyone can detect the stink!

HEY, GUY RAZ, WHAT'S GROSSER THAN GROSS?

YOUR COLLECTION OF USED BAND-AIDS?

GUY RAZ, IN ANCIENT ROME, PEOPLE USED TO BRUSH THEIR TEETH WITH PEE BECAUSE THEY THOUGHT IT WOULD GIVE THEM A BRIGHTER, WHITER SMILE!

YOU'RE NOT GOING TO TRY THIS, ARE YOU?

WHAT?! NO! THERE'S NOT EVEN ANY SCIENTIFIC EVIDENCE TO BACK IT UP.

WELL, DO YOU KNOW WHAT'S GROSSER THAN GROSS?

THE BIRD OVER THERE BARFING INTO HER BABY BIRD'S MOUTH?

MINDY, THE US ARMY MANUAL ADVISES AGAINST DRINKING URINE IN A SURVIVAL SITUATION BECAUSE IT'S SALTY AND WOULD PROBABLY MAKE YOUR CONDITION EVEN WORSE.

WHAT?! THE ARMY HAS TO SPECIFICALLY TELL TROOPS NOT TO DRINK THEIR OWN PEE?

ANYTHING FOR SURVIVAL! I THINK THEY JUST LIKE TO BE PREPARED.

Fact Snacks

★ On average, people pee between six and seven times per day. (When was the last time *you* counted?)

★ People tend to pee *more* as they age. (It's good to have things to look forward to!)

★ For most people, a good healthy pee lasts between 8 and 34 seconds. (Time it next time!)

What Is the Color of My Pee Telling Me?

After you pee and before you flush, take a moment to observe your latest toilet deposit. Believe it or not, the color of your pee can tell you a thing or two about your overall health. Bookmark this page for some light bathroom reading and refer to this chart as a guide.

Clear ➡ You're a real overachiever in the hydration department. You may want to back off the water until your pee is the color of a cool pale yellow.

Pale yellow ➡ If Goldilocks were looking in your toilet, she'd proclaim this one as "Juuuuust right." High fives for proper hydration!

Dark yellow ➡ Does the color of your pee remind you of honey? Well, it shouldn't. Go pour yourself a glass of water and let your body do its thing.

GOLDILOCKS AND THE THREE TOILETS

BODY PART AWARDS

BONUS BODY
BODY PART AWARDS

PLEASE JOIN US AS WE ROLL OUT THE RED CARPET FOR THE BIGGEST, SMALLEST, SHORTEST, AND STRONGEST OF YOUR HUMAN BODY!

FIRST UP WE BRING YOU **SKIN**!

JUST LOOK AT THAT SKIN STRUT IT'S STUFF!

TONIGHT SKIN WILL BE RECEIVING THE AWARD FOR **BIGGEST ORGAN OF THE HUMAN BODY!**

SKIN IS AN ORGAN WORN ON THE OUTSIDE OF THE HUMAN BODY, AND ON ADULTS IT WEIGHS AROUND 8 POUNDS AND IT'S ABOUT 22 SQUARE FEET LONG!

AND LOOK AT HOW FANTASTIC IT LOOKS DRAPED OVER THE HUMAN BODY!

AND THAT'S NOT ALL, GUY RAZ! WITHOUT SKIN, WE WOULD LITERALLY EVAPORATE! LET'S GIVE IT UP FOR SKIN!

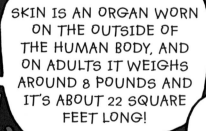

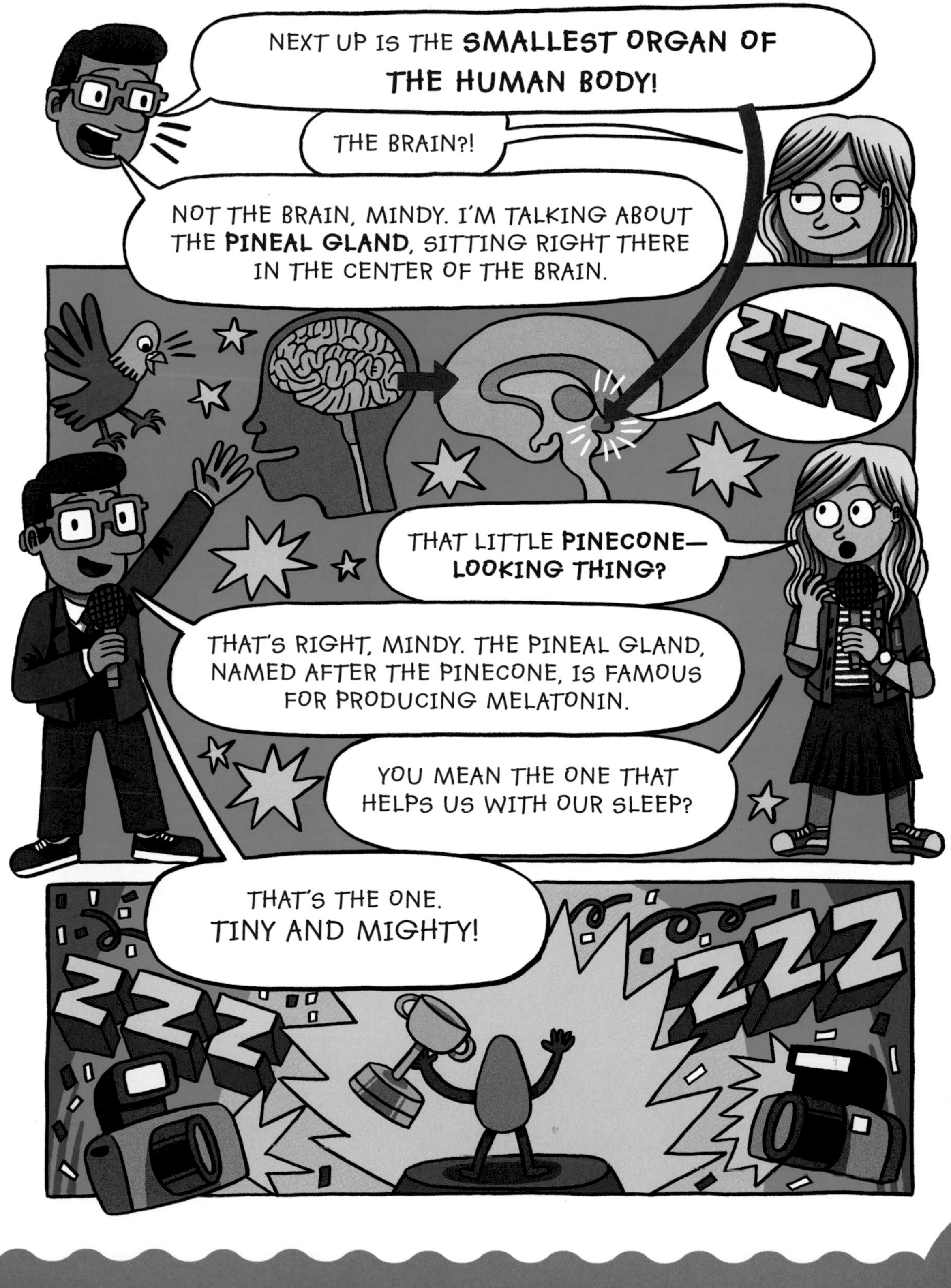
NEXT UP IS THE **SMALLEST ORGAN OF THE HUMAN BODY!**
THE BRAIN?!
NOT THE BRAIN, MINDY. I'M TALKING ABOUT THE **PINEAL GLAND**, SITTING RIGHT THERE IN THE CENTER OF THE BRAIN.
ZZZ
THAT LITTLE **PINECONE—LOOKING THING?**
THAT'S RIGHT, MINDY. THE PINEAL GLAND, NAMED AFTER THE PINECONE, IS FAMOUS FOR PRODUCING MELATONIN.
YOU MEAN THE ONE THAT HELPS US WITH OUR SLEEP?
THAT'S THE ONE. TINY AND MIGHTY!
ZZZ
ZZZ

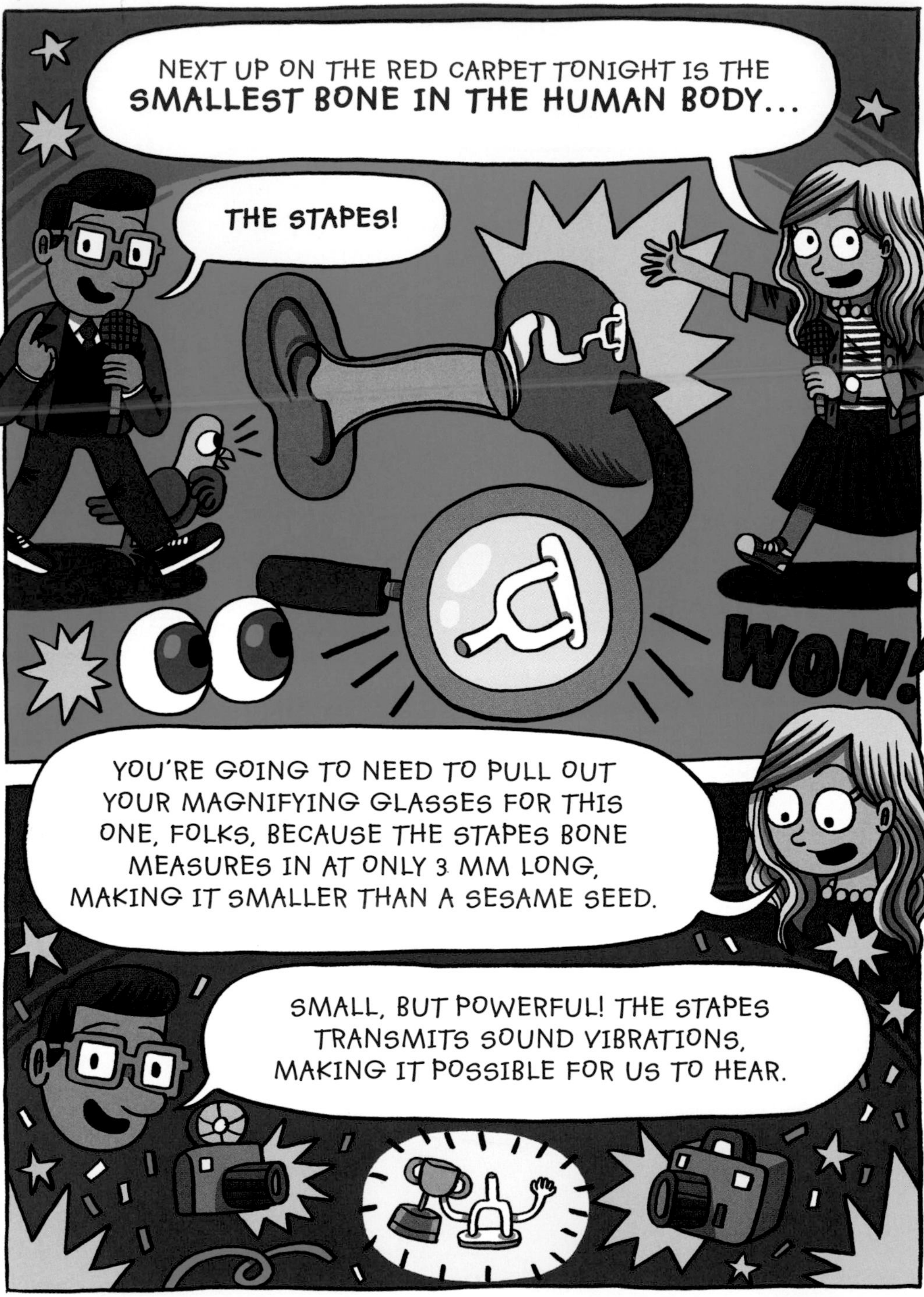
NEXT UP ON THE RED CARPET TONIGHT IS THE SMALLEST BONE IN THE HUMAN BODY...
THE STAPES!
WOW!
YOU'RE GOING TO NEED TO PULL OUT YOUR MAGNIFYING GLASSES FOR THIS ONE, FOLKS, BECAUSE THE STAPES BONE MEASURES IN AT ONLY 3 MM LONG, MAKING IT SMALLER THAN A SESAME SEED.
SMALL, BUT POWERFUL! THE STAPES TRANSMITS SOUND VIBRATIONS, MAKING IT POSSIBLE FOR US TO HEAR.

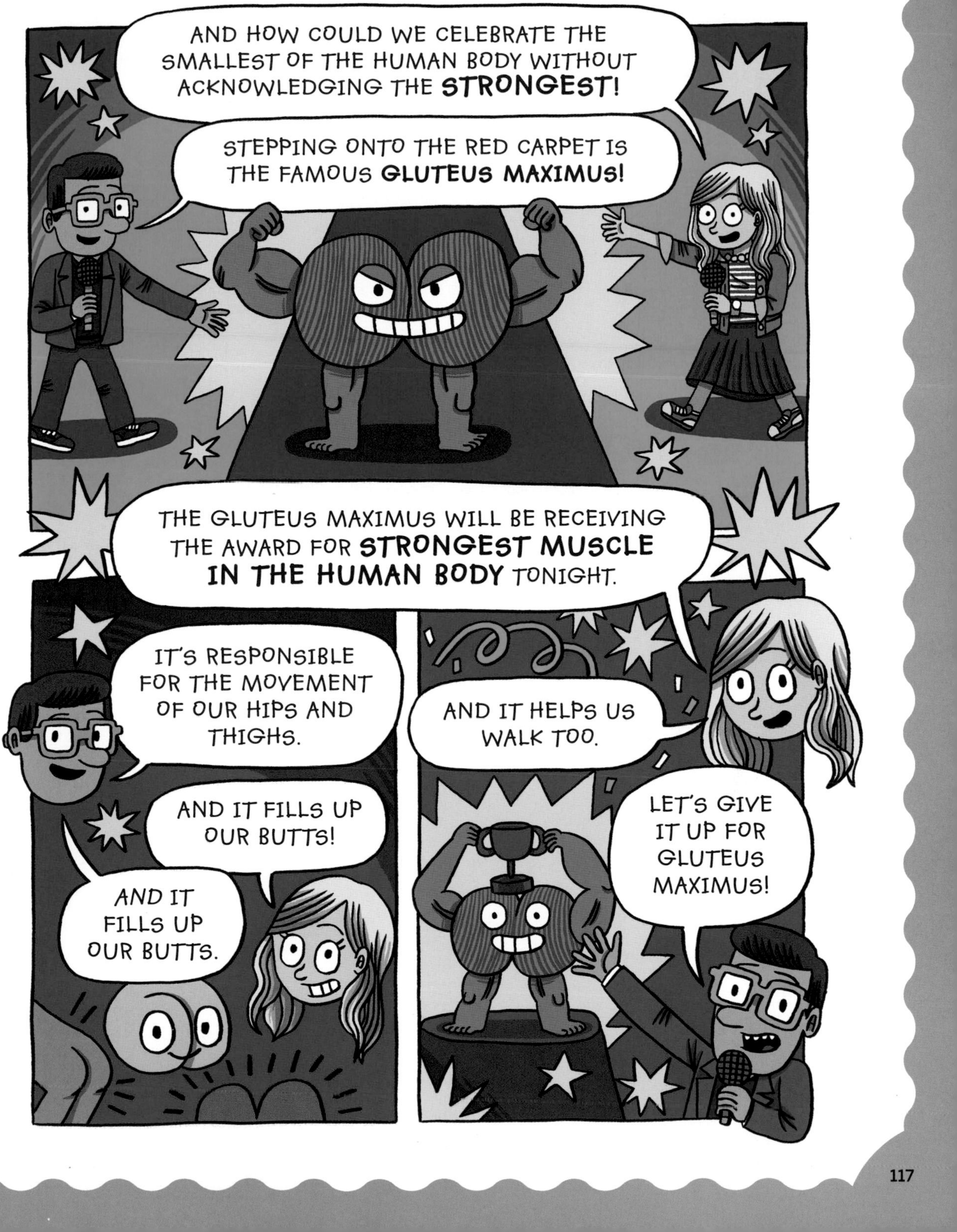
AND HOW COULD WE CELEBRATE THE SMALLEST OF THE HUMAN BODY WITHOUT ACKNOWLEDGING THE STRONGEST!
STEPPING ONTO THE RED CARPET IS THE FAMOUS GLUTEUS MAXIMUS!
THE GLUTEUS MAXIMUS WILL BE RECEIVING THE AWARD FOR STRONGEST MUSCLE IN THE HUMAN BODY TONIGHT.
IT'S RESPONSIBLE FOR THE MOVEMENT OF OUR HIPS AND THIGHS.
AND IT FILLS UP OUR BUTTS!
AND IT FILLS UP OUR BUTTS.
AND IT HELPS US WALK TOO.
LET'S GIVE IT UP FOR GLUTEUS MAXIMUS!

DIGESTION

HOW TO TRANSFORM YOUR FOOD INTO POOP!

Digestion
Taking a Ride Down the Digestive Slide

Poop
The Scoop on Poop

The Gas Station
Tooting Your Own Horn

DIGESTIÓN

Taking a Ride Down the Digestive Slide

What goes in must come out—as *poop*. But what kind of wild ride does your food experience before it re-emerges on the other end in a form that is completely unrecognizable? It's time to talk digestion, the twenty-four-plus-hour process of turning food into fuel for your body.

Before your body can use the food you eat for energy and fuel, it must first break it down. Once that happens, your body can suck out all the nutrients and pack itself with all the power you need to get through the day.

How to Digest Your Food

Step 1: What's That Smell? Before food even enters your mouth, digestion can begin. All you need is something to trigger your sense of smell, causing you to salivate. Fresh-baked cookies, movie theater popcorn, dripped cheese burning on the bottom of the oven—what makes *your* mouth water?

Step 2: Time to Eat! Take a bite and chew that food to bits. Tear it to shreds! (Keep your mouth closed. No one wants to see what is happening inside that thing!) Your spit is adding a slippery coating to every bite, making it easy to swallow, while an enzyme called amylase starts to break down the carbohydrates and sugars in your mouth before they even reach your stomach.

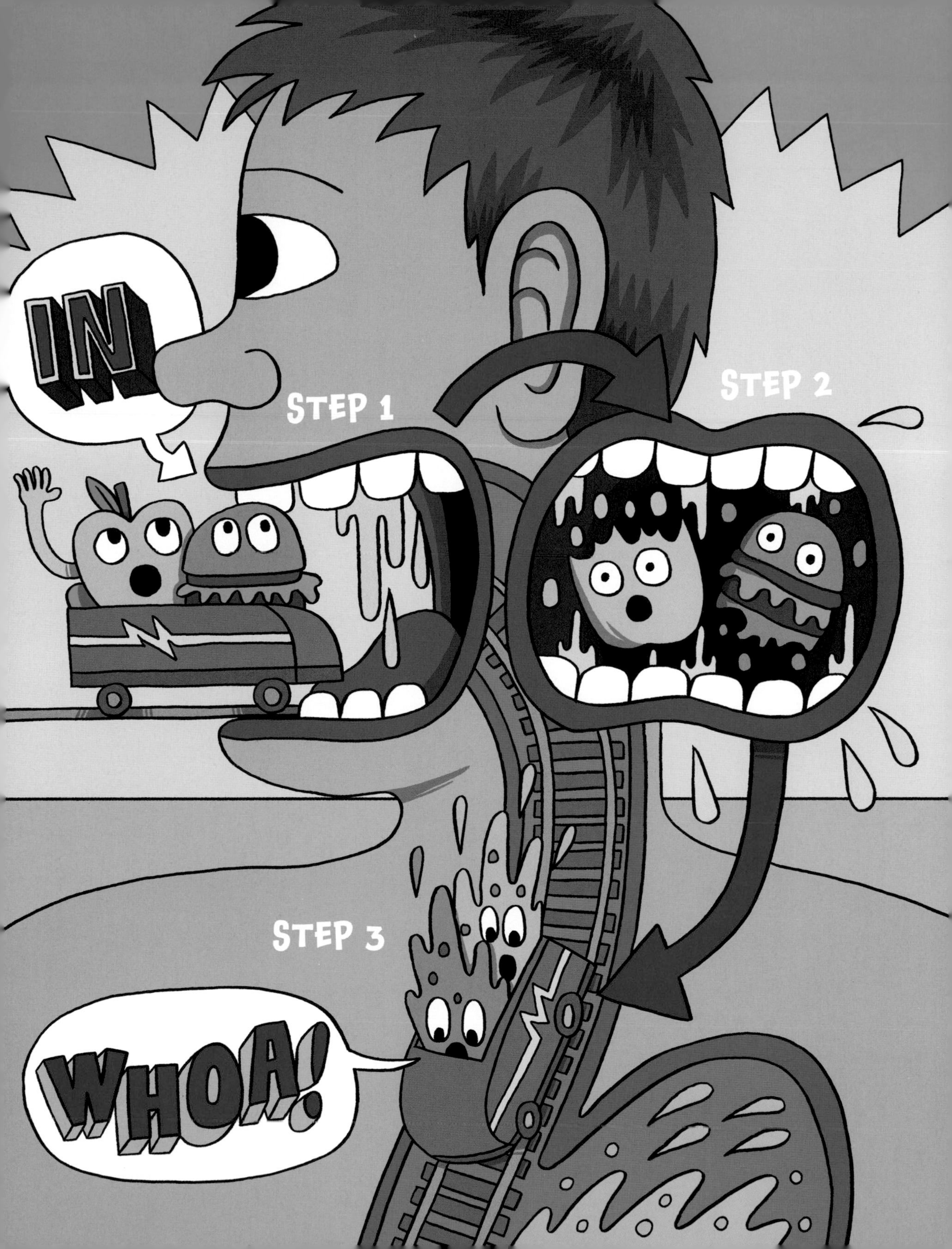
IN
STEP 1
STEP 2
STEP 3
WHOA!

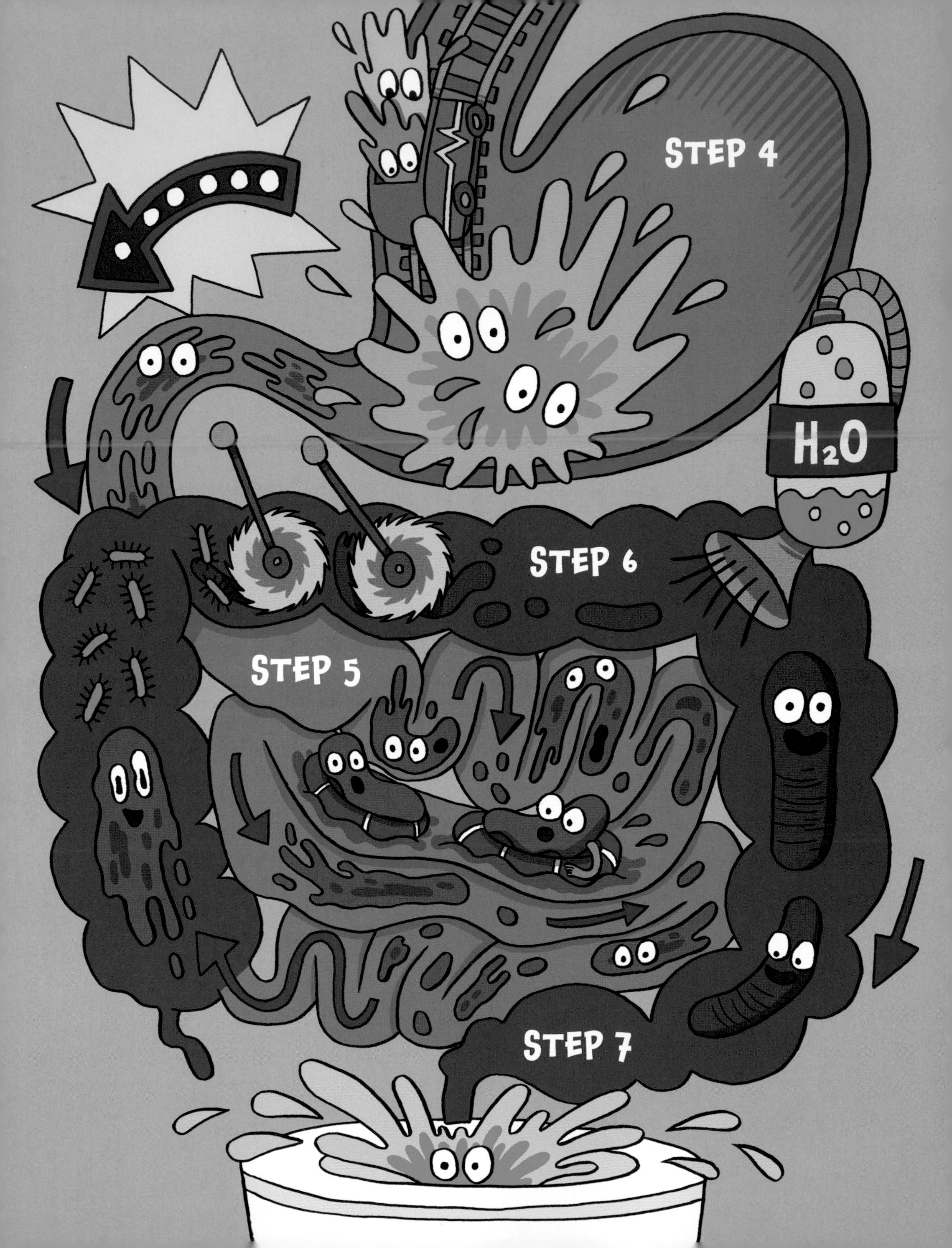
STEP 4
H_2O
STEP 6
STEP 5
STEP 7

Step 3: Push & Swallow As you swallow, your food moves its way down a long hallway known as the esophagus. Once it's there, your throat muscles kick in to help push it all the way through to your stomach.

FACT

Did you know that you can swallow even while doing a headstand or hanging upside down like a bat? Food doesn't need gravity's help to work its way into your stomach!

Step 4: It's Tummy Time! At this point, your food has made its way into your stomach, where it is greeted with a bunch of bodily juices and muscles that work to churn it, mix it, and break it down even further. And thanks to a little ring of muscle called the sphincter, this is also food's point of no return! If your food even thinks about going back up to where it came from, the sphincter will squeeze the point where your stomach meets your esophagus shut and keep it from heading in the wrong direction.

FACT

Your stomach is coated in a thick layer of mucus to protect it from its own stomach acids, which could otherwise cause it to digest itself.

Step 5: Let's Begin with the Small Intestine By now, your food has been transformed into a thick liquid, just the right consistency to move through your small intestine. Teeny-tiny finger-like bits called villi are waiting along its walls. The villi hand off nutrients to your blood, which then delivers the nutrients to the rest of your body. Your small intestine is where most of the digestion magic happens.

FACT

The small intestine is about twenty feet (6 m) long and one inch (2.5 cm) wide!

Step 6: Let's Make Some Poop!

At this point, the nutrients from your small intestine are all absorbed by your blood, happily fueling the rest of your body. But what about the waste?! Time to move into the large intestine. Your large intestine is sucking out the leftover water and mixing the undigested food with bacteria, drying it out, and using these ingredients to make stone-cold, solid-gold, grade A POOP!

Step 7: Last Stop Before Toilet Town

After a long twenty-four-plus-hour ride, your food is digested and your body is fueled. At this point, your poop is ready to leave the station. But what if *you're* not ready?! Lucky for you, your body has a built-in waiting room for poop. It's called the rectum, and it's a little muscular chamber that holds your poop until you're ready to push it out. *But don't wait too long.* There's more poop on the way, and you don't want to cause any backups!

124

Tummy Aches

A lot of things can give you a tummy ache. In fact, it's just another way for your body to send a message telling you something is wrong. While things like stressful emotions or constipation could cause a tummy ache, the most common culprit is gastrointestinal disturbance, AKA there's something funky in your stomach. This could mean something that you're allergic to or bad bacteria that somehow gets in there. But lucky for you, your body has a backup plan! Unfortunately, that backup plan may sometimes involve barf and/or diarrhea. But on the bright side, those two powerful forces have the ability to expel the intruders, getting them out of there for good.

P.O.O.P.

The Scoop on Poop

DEAR DIARY, GOOD POOP TODAY! IT WAS LUMPY...

WEIGHT COLOR SHAPE

What Kind of Poo Are You? The Bristol Stool Scale

In 1997, Dr. Ken Heaton, from the University of Bristol in the UK, successfully potty-trained sixty-six volunteers to poop for science. Each of these volunteers changed their daily diets, swallowed special marker pellets, and kept a diary (yes, a *diary*) of their individual poops. Dr. Heaton then took these diary entries and came up with the Bristol Stool Scale, AKA the Meyers Scale, AKA the Poop Chart!

Why a chart? Pooping is [supposed to be] easy, but talking about it can be hard. Dr. Heaton wanted to help patients better describe the shapes and types of their poops to their doctors. The chart is also designed to help doctors diagnose potential digestive problems. Talk about taking toilet talk to new heights!

TYPE 1: LITTLE, HARD, AND LUMPY POOP NUGGETS THAT HURT AS THEY MAKE THEIR WAY INTO THE WORLD

★ Could be a sign of constipation.

TYPE 2: LUMPY SAUSAGE POOP

★ Another sign of constipation!

TYPE 3: SAUSAGE LOG FULL OF CRACKS

★ Did you push out this poop in one minute or less?

★ Was it soft and easy to pass?

★ If you answered yes to both of these questions, congratulations! You've got yourself a healthy poop! Flush, wash your hands, and have a nice day!

TYPE 4: LONG, SMOOTH, SAUSAGE SNAKE

★ This is a grade A poop right here!
If only all poops could be so smooth
and easy. Aim for dropping out one
of these babies every one to three days!

TYPE 5: BLOBBY POOP NUGGETS WITH CLEAR EDGES

★ Good news: Easy on the exit

★ Bad news: They knock without
warning and could be a sign that
diarrhea is coming to visit.

TYPE 6: FLUFFY, MUSHY, AND FRAYED

★ Three or more of these in a
single day, and you are definitely
dunkin' some diarrhea. Be sure
to drink plenty of water and drinks
containing electrolytes.

TYPE 7: POOP SOUP

★ If your poop is fast, furious, and almost entirely liquid, it's most definitely diarrhea. And if it lasts for more than two days, you should talk to your grownup about going to see a doctor, as diarrhea can cause dehydration.

TYPE 1 & 2

You're doing the Constipation Conga

TYPE 3 & 4

You're dancing with some Super Duper Poop

TYPE 5, 6 & 7

You're doing the Diarrhea Disco

ASK WOW

DEAR WOW IN THE WORLD,

THE CORN I ATE FOR DINNER LAST NIGHT RESURFACED IN MY POOP THIS MORNING. SHOULD I BE WORRIED?

SINCERELY,
PARTY POOPCORN

DEAR PARTY POOPCORN,
FINDING CORN IN YOUR POOP IS PERFECTLY NORMAL (UNLESS YOU HAVEN'T BEEN EATING CORN!). SEE, CORN HAS A SHELL MADE OF CELLULOSE, A FIBROUS PLANT MATERIAL THAT'S SUPER HEALTHY FOR US TO EAT, BUT ULTIMATELY UNDIGESTIBLE FOR US HUMANS. NOTHING TO WORRY ABOUT!

DEAR MINDY & GUY RAZ,

SOMETIMES MY POOP FLOATS LIKE A BOAT, AND SOMETIMES IT SINKS LIKE A LOG. WHY DOES THIS HAPPEN?

SIGNED,
CONFUSED & AMUSED

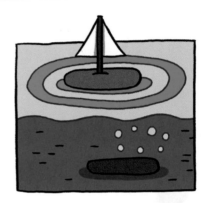

DEAR CONFUSED & AMUSED,
A HEALTHY POOP SHOULD LOOK LIKE ONE OR TWO GOOD-SIZE SUNKEN LOGS. FLOATING POOP COULD BE A SIGN THAT YOU'RE NOT GETTING THE RIGHT NUTRIENTS, OR THAT YOU'RE SUPER GASSY. SO IF YOU'RE EXPERIENCING MORE FLOATERS THAN SINKERS, TALK TO A GROWNUP ABOUT GETTING A LITTLE MORE FIBER IN YOUR DAILY DIET.

ASK WOW

DEAR WOW IN THE WORLD,

POOP LOOKS LIKE CHOCOLATE, BUT IT DOESN'T TASTE LIKE CHOCOLATE. IF POOP ISN'T CHOCOLATE, THEN WHAT IS IT?

WANTING ANSWERS,
A PERSON WHO DEFINITELY DOESN'T KNOW THIS FROM FIRSTHAND EXPERIENCE

DEAR A PERSON WHO DEFINITELY DOESN'T KNOW THIS FROM FIRSTHAND EXPERIENCE,

YOU'RE RIGHT! DESPITE THEIR SOMETIMES UNCANNY RESEMBLANCE, POOP AND CHOCOLATE ARE TWO VERY, VERY, VERY...VERY DIFFERENT THINGS. CHOCOLATE IS MADE PRIMARILY OF CACAO BEANS AND SUGAR, WHEREAS POOP IS MADE OF A WHOLE HOST OF DIFFERENT INGREDIENTS: 75 PERCENT WATER AND 25 PERCENT DEAD BACTERIA, INDIGESTIBLE FOOD MATTER, FATS, PROTEIN, AND A BUNCH OF OTHER STUFF (IN MUCH SMALLER AMOUNTS) THAT IS DECIDEDLY NOT FOUND IN CHOCOLATE. IN SHORT, POOP IS BASICALLY JUST ALL THE STUFF THAT'S LEFT OVER ONCE YOUR DIGESTIVE SYSTEM (STOMACH, SMALL INTESTINE, LARGE INTESTINE) ABSORBS THE NUTRIENTS AND FLUIDS FROM WHAT YOU EAT AND DRINK, LIKE CHOCOLATE! OR CHOCOLATE MILK!

Potty Training

According to a 2003 study, our bodies are not designed to sit while we poop. In fact, getting squatty while we go potty is the way to go. Literally. You see, there's a little kink in our lower gut. This kink is what helps keep the poop from just randomly falling out of our bodies. However, when we squat, our gut straightens out, allowing the poop to comfortably sliiiiiiiide out at a speed of approximately eighty seconds faster than it does when we sit. That's some serious speed pooping!

How to Poop . . . According to Science

OPTION A

Step 1: Climb on top of the toilet and perch yourself into a squat on the seat.

Step 2: For the next fifty-one seconds, enjoy the speed of expulsion.

Time out! Perch yourself on the potty? That sounds dangerous.

Okay, fine. Option B.

OPTION B

Step 1: Get yourself a little stool, place it in front of the toilet, and elevate your feet.

Step 2: You know what to doo-doo.

Step 3: Give a round of applause for science!

Step 4: Flush!

Step 5: Wash your hands!

Happy Fifty-Thousandth Birthday, Poop!

While we don't know the actual drop date of the oldest human poop ever found, we do know that it first made its way into the world about fifty thousand years ago! By the time it was discovered by archaeologists in Spain, it was completely fossilized, making it rock-solid and odorless. Scientists were able to determine that it belonged to a Neanderthal, a completely separate species from modern humans like us. It also provided some of the first evidence that along with meat, berries, and nuts, Neanderthals ate their veggies! Do you?

Perhaps this story will inspire you to save *your* poop for future generations to find, and to that we say, PLEASE DON'T.

Tooting Your Own Horn

When you eat, you're actually swallowing more than just your food. With every bite, you're also ingesting air—and that air contains gas. As this food and gas work their way through your digestive system, they're broken down in your large intestine, where they make even more gas. SO MUCH GAS! Your body can't possibly contain it all, so it's got to find an escape route. You don't need us to tell you where that is. But we'll tell you anyway: YOUR BUTT! Gases escaping from your butt are called farts, or, scientifically speaking, flatus (FLAY-tus). The word "flatus" sounds like a fancy, formal fart, don't you think?

WOULD YOU BE SO KIND AS TO PLEASE PASS THE FLATUS?

TOOT!

THE AROMA!

VERBS(ish)

CUT THE
CHEESE,
BREAK WIND,
PASS GAS,
FIRE A STINK
TORPEDO,
POP A FLUFFY,
BLAST THE
BUTT TUBA

NOUN OR VERB

FART, TOOT,
POOT, BEEF

NOUNS

STINKER,
BUTT BURP,
VAPOR LOAF,
STINK BISCUIT,
MOUSE ON
A
MOTORCYCLE

DON'T TRY THIS AT HOME EXPERIMENT

Farts

Yields: One Fabulous Fragrant Fart

Ingredients

Hydrogen

Carbon dioxide

Methane mixed with hydrogen sulfide and ammonia

Directions

Mix these ingredients in a large intestine. Toot it out your
buns. Inhale through your nose at your own risk. Send a
complaint/compliment letter to our editor for allowing us
to publish this toxic/aromatic recipe for stink biscuits:

Amy Cloud—Children's Book Editor

Houghton Mifflin Harcourt Publishing

3 Park Avenue

New York, NY 10016

Fart Fact Snacks

★ The average healthy person farts between fourteen and twenty times a day.

★ Farts can travel up to ten feet (3 m) per second. That's seven miles per hour (11 kmph)! Think you can outrun a fart? Try it!

★ Girls fart as much as boys.

★ Moms vs. dads: there is evidence that men fart more than women, and that female farts tend to smell worse. Do I smell a science experiment?

★ Good news: holding in a fart will not cause you to explode. Bad news: holding in a fart could give you a stomachache.

WIND-BREAKING WOW!

The Guinness World Record for the Loudest Recorded Burp was awarded to a man named **Paul Hunn**, of the UK, in 2009. The record-breaking burp clocked in at 109.9 decibels. That's almost two decibels louder than a chainsaw!

List of People Who Fart

Spend some time thinking of each one of these *fartastic* people in your life!

Teachers

Librarians

Babies

Grandmas

Presidents

Dogs
(okay, technically not people, but you'd never know it by the smell of their toots!)

The authors of this book

News anchors

Every person you'll ever know

Burps

A burp (okay, some people call it a belch, but we are not those people) is just a not-at-all fancy word for GAS. And like a fart, a burp is caused by swallowing air that contains gases when we eat or drink. But unlike a fart, a burp never makes its way to the large intestine. Instead, it's pushed out of the stomach, up through the esophagus, and out the mouth in the form of a BURRRRRRP!

How to Feel like You're Falling through the Floor without Falling through the Floor

Step 1: Lie on your belly.

Step 2: Have a friend gently pull the top half of your body up by holding you by the wrists. Keep your head and body relaxed.

Step 3: Keep this going for thirty seconds. "ONE *Wow in the World*, TWO *Wow in the Worlds*, THREE *Wow in the Worlds* . . ."

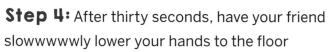

Step 4: After thirty seconds, have your friend slowwwwwly lower your hands to the floor

WHAT JUST HAPPENED?! As your arms were lowered, you felt like you were *falling through the floor!* OH, SILLY BODY AND BRAIN!

How to Use Your Hands as a Calculator

Assuming you have ten fingers, your hands can help you multiply by nine. Let's try it using 6 × 9.

Step 1: Display both hands out in front of you and put down the finger that corresponds with the number you're multiplying by 9.

Step 2: The number of fingers to the left of your lowered finger is the first digit of the answer (5), and the number of fingers to the right of that lowered finger is the second digit of the answer (4).

Step 3: Put them together and the answer is 54!   **6x9=54**

How to Stop Brain Freeze

Brain freeze is our body's way of telling us to CHILL OUT when we attempt to eat frozen foods or drinks too fast. But lucky for you, there's a way to hack it. Here's how:

Step 1: Put down the ice cream.

Step 2: Press your tongue against the roof of your mouth, warming up that soft palate.

Step 3: Keep the pressure up until the brain freeze subsides.

Step 4: Go back to enjoying your ice cream. Slowwwwly.

Step 5: Check out the *Wow in the World* podcast episode called "Brain Freeze"!

THE IMMUNE SYSTEM

Siiiiick

THE IMMUNE SYSTEM

SIIIIICK

Every day, microscopic invaders attempt to work their way into your body with the sole intention of making you *sick*. Luckily for you, your body has built-in defenses ready to take on those invaders faster than you can say "ACHOO"!

The P-Team (P Stands for Pathogen)

Let's meet some infamous body invaders!

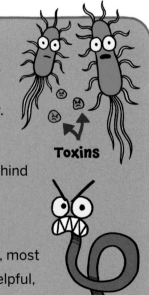

Bacteria!

DETAILS: They have the power to multiply rapidly. A few can cause serious diseases by invading the body. Some can release harmful molecules called toxins.

Toxins

KNOWN FOR: Bacteria are the infamous villains behind diseases such as strep throat, urinary tract infections, and food poisoning.

HIDDEN TALENT: Not *all* bacteria are bad. In fact, most are pretty harmless. And some bacteria are actually helpful, like the kind in your gut that help digest your food.

Viruses!

DETAILS: They reproduce by invading a body cell. Once inside, they turn the hijacked cell into a factory where more viruses are made and released to infect more cells.

KNOWN FOR: Viruses are the infamous villains behind hits such as the common cold, the flu, and cold sores.

HIDDEN TALENT: Most viruses are just bad to the bone and looking for trouble.

When a Virus Goes Viral

In early 2020, we—people all around the world—found ourselves in something called a "global pandemic." A pandemic is an outbreak of a disease that makes its way across an entire country or even the world. In a pandemic, a disease that can cause some people to be seriously sick, like the new coronavirus, which causes COVID-19, spreads easily from person to person. This makes it difficult to control and contain without the help of a protective vaccine or cure. Think of a pandemic as a game of tag that NO ONE wants to play, but where you can mark yourself "not it!" by sitting out, washing your hands, and wearing a mask. Protecting ourselves and one another is the name of the game!

The B-Team (B Stands for Body Barriers)

Now let's meet your body's first responders: the body barriers! Bacteria, viruses, and other pathogens have plenty of sneaky ways of intruding your body. From hitching a ride on the food you eat to disguising themselves in the air you breathe, they'll stop at almost nothing to ruin your day. And that's where your body barriers step in on the front lines of defense!

Tears

Most pathogens don't stand a chance against the salty tears waiting to wash them away once and for all.

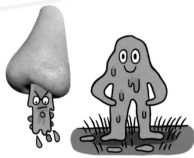

Mucus

Lining your nose and ready to trap germs with its super-stick power!

Saliva

This slimy spit is chemical-filled and ready to kill—mouth germs, that is!

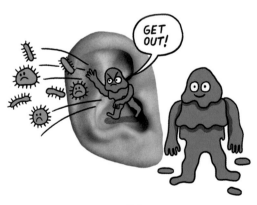

GET OUT!

Wax

Thick and sticky and scaring away ear invaders since the dawn of . . . ears?

Skin

A full-body suit of armor guarding you against infection.

Blood

Different types of white blood cells unite to attack invaders both inside and outside the body.

Stomach

Deploying powerful acid to destroy the germs you ate.

Help You Be a Healthy You!

But the greatest human body first responder of all time is . . . *you!* And here are your not-so-secret weapons:

Soap and water: By washing your hands before you eat and after you use the toilet, you're washing away those sneaky germs trying to invade your body.

Let your doctor help you! Whether it's encouraging you to say YES to vaccine shots or to eat veggies, your doctor's job is to help you help yourself stay healthy!

Keep your fingers out of your nose, eyes, and mouth: Do you know where your fingers have been?! Stop hand-delivering germs to the rest of your body!

THE REPRODUCTIVE SYSTEM

HOW HUMANS MAKE HUMANS

The Circle of Life

Let's Explore!

Puberty

Whaterty?

THE CIRCLE OF LIFE

Let's Explore!

The human body is capable of doing some truly incredible things. It can heal its own bones, recognize at least a million different shades of colors, and create a new layer of skin every month! But perhaps one of the most amazing things the body can do is *make other humans!*

Introducing . . . the reproductive system! Adults have special cells that work together to create human life. The male cells are called sperm, and the female cells are called eggs.

Both are required when it comes to making a human baby. First the male cell (sperm) must find a female cell (egg) and join forces. This process is known as fertilization, and it all happens inside the woman's uterus. After an egg is fertilized, an embryo is formed. This embryo will grow and develop in that same stretchy uterus for the next nine months until *DING* OUT COMES A BABY!

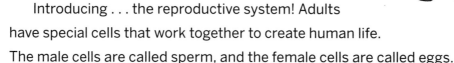

TEAMWORK!

IT'S A BABY!

9 MONTHS PASS

THAT BABY TURNED INTO A KID!

SPERM AND EGG MEET!

PUBERTY!

THAT ADULT FINDS ANOTHER ADULT!

THAT KID TURNED INTO AN ADULT!

Since you're a kid, your reproductive system is still under construction, and that's okay because you won't be needing it anytime soon. However, sometime between the ages of eight and fifteen,* your body will begin going through some big changes both inside and out as you move from a kid to an adult! These changes are known as puberty.

* Puberty tends to occur earlier for girls, happening anywhere between eight and thirteen years old. For many boys, puberty hits one to three years later, between the ages of nine and fifteen.

Whaterty?

PUBERTY! (That's pronounced PEE-YOU-birdy, not POO-birdy.) Go ahead, say it out loud. It's kind of a funny word for some people, but also a good one to get used to: you're going to be hearing it *a lot* more as you get older.

So what changes are we talking here?

Biologically speaking, there are some big differences between boys and girls in terms of the way their reproductive systems are formed. For example, during this time, girls' bodies will begin to release eggs and boys' bodies will begin to produce sperm. Girls will notice bumps on their chests in the form of breasts and boys will notice as their larynx grows, forming an Adam's apple on their necks.

But that's not all!

Changes that both boys *and* girls get to look forward to include (but are not limited to) the following:

Ready . . . Set . . . Grow! Expect a rapid growth spurt of up to four inches (10 cm) in just one year! By the time your growth spurt ends, you'll have reached your maximum adult height (or just about). During this time, your body will grow in other ways too. Boys may notice wider shoulders and larger muscles, girls may notice wider hips and larger developing breasts, and everyone can count on a little extra clumsiness. It's going to take you and your brain some time to adjust to your rapidly changing bod!

Hello, Hormones! Puberty hormones are the little chemical messengers that will be running throughout your body, commanding your cells. Depending on the stage of puberty you're in, you may experience more or less of these hormones. And while you can't *see* the hormones, they have plenty of sneaky ways to make themselves known.

Pimples: Pimples or acne are the little red bumps that you may experience during puberty. They usually pop up on your face, but don't be surprised if you find them on your chest or back too. These bumps are caused by the newly turbocharged oil glands on your skin. Dead skin cells get caught in the extra oil, making a gross gunk that clogs up your pores and forms tiny infections. Pimples might not be considered a perk of puberty, but they are a perfectly normal part of growing up.

Emotional Roller Coaster: During puberty, your hormone levels will be bouncing up and down like a bunch of bonkerballs. One minute you're laughing, the next minute you're crying. And to top it all off, your brain has decided to make all sorts of changes to the parts that deal with emotions. UGHHHHHH! So saddle up and endure the ride! (*Psst* . . . all your peers will be on it too.)

Snore More: When it comes time for puberty, you're going to need even more sleep than you need now. A hormone called melatonin will usually be released later into the night than it is now, making it later to bed, harder to rise. Give your teenage self a good bedtime!

Hair?!? THERE?!? If there's one thing puberty can't get enough of, it's *hair*. And you're going to start finding it everywhere! Or at least, it may feel like it at first. Boys and girls may notice hair sprouting in different spots, but everyone can look forward to finding it in their armpits. Add a couple of googly eyes* and you've got your own personal puberty monster! *not recommended

Who Dropped the BASS?! During puberty, you might start to notice a lump on your throat, especially if you're a boy. *Don't freak out.* This is simply the result of your larynx growing to make room for your thicker vocal cords! This lump is what makes up your Adam's apple, and as it forms, your voice will begin to sound deeper. You can thank the ol' testosterone hormone for this one. Also, as you get used to your thicker vocal cords, you may notice your voice cracking back into your old kid voice. Think of it as your kid self just popping in to say hi!

By the time you've finished puberty, your body should have a fully functioning reproductive system. And while biologically speaking it will be ready to make humans, the decision to do that will come much later in your life! Babies require a lot of time, patience, money, and diapers. Four things that you don't have right now! Did we mention that babies poop and drool almost 24/7?

It's a BOY! It's a GIRL! It's ... to BE DETERMINED. Or NOT!

Not all babies are born boys or girls, males or females. There are actually many more ways of being a person than most people realize! For example, some people are born with reproductive parts that don't necessarily match the specific characteristics of "male" or "female." Others, as they grow, may find that they don't identify with the "boy" or "girl" label they were given the day they were born. It's important to remember that the human race is a variety pack of nearly eight *billion* people, and no two are exactly alike. Pretty *wow* just to be human, huh?

 START! YOUR BRAIN SIGNALS IT'S GO TIME!

 GROWTH SPURT! MOVE 4 INCHES AHEAD.

 MOOD SWINGS SWING AHEAD 3 SPACES AND THEN SWING BACK 6 MORE.

 SNOOZE CITY LOSE YOUR TURN AND GET MORE SLEEP!

 UH OH! LACK OF JUDGMENT. DECISION-MAKING PART OF THE BRAIN IS STILL UNDER CONSTRUCTION. GO BACK TO START.

 THE LUMPS SURPRISE! YOUR LUMPS HAVE ARRIVED!

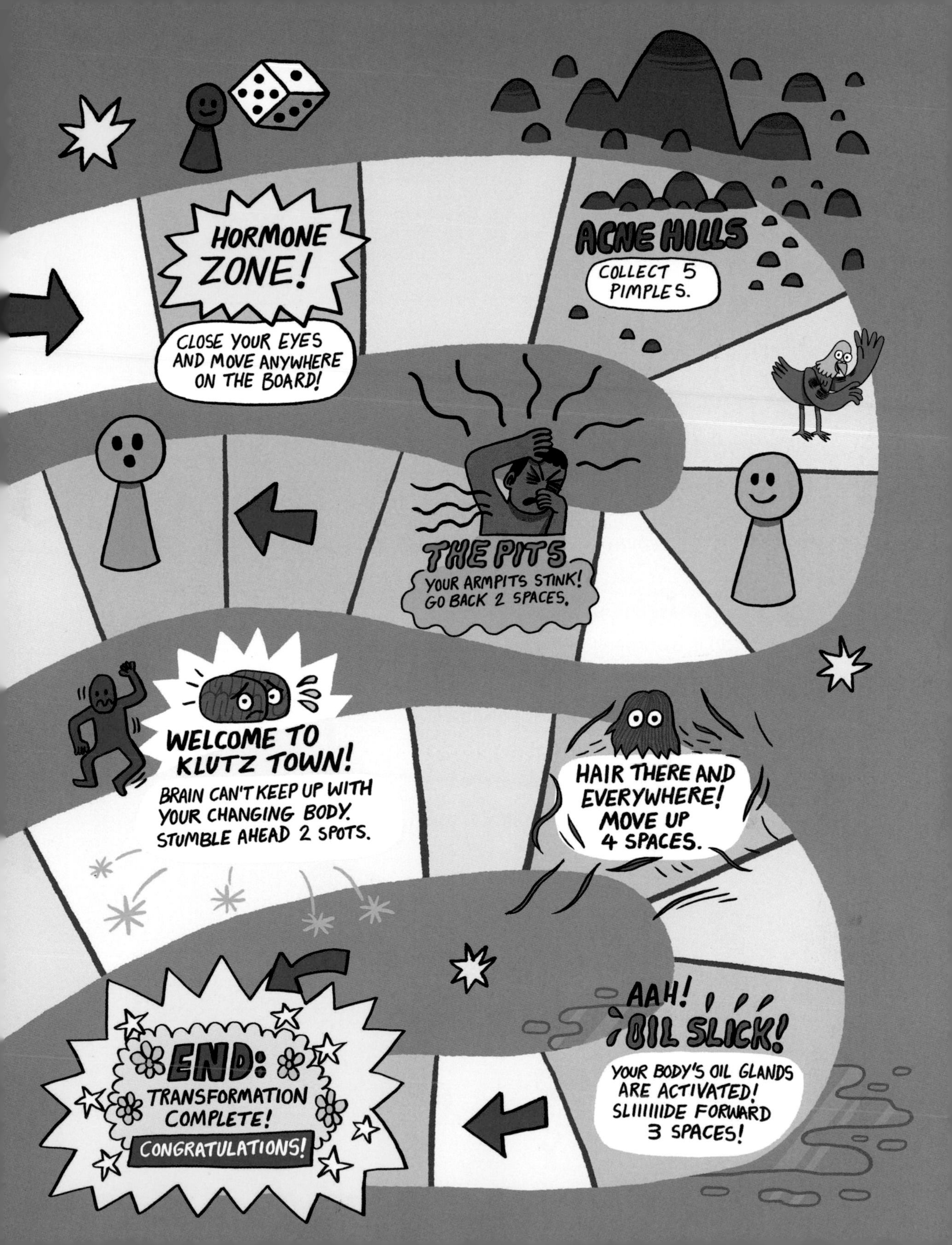
HORMONE ZONE!
CLOSE YOUR EYES AND MOVE ANYWHERE ON THE BOARD!
ACNE HILLS
COLLECT 5 PIMPLES.
THE PITS
YOUR ARMPITS STINK! GO BACK 2 SPACES.
WELCOME TO KLUTZ TOWN!
BRAIN CAN'T KEEP UP WITH YOUR CHANGING BODY. STUMBLE AHEAD 2 SPOTS.
HAIR THERE AND EVERYWHERE! MOVE UP 4 SPACES.
AAH!
OIL SLICK!
YOUR BODY'S OIL GLANDS ARE ACTIVATED! SLIIIIIIDE FORWARD 3 SPACES!
END:
TRANSFORMATION COMPLETE!
CONGRATULATIONS!

BONUS BODY

THE BUTT

Guess what? Even this book has a butt!

The butt, or buttocks, is defined as "the two round fleshy parts that form the lower rear area of a human trunk." And every human has a pair of buttocks. Can't find your gluteus maximus? We'll give you a clue: you're sitting on it!

The gluteus maximus is located underneath a layer of fat and is the largest and most powerful gravity-defying muscle in your body. Without the gluteus maximus, you would not be able to climb stairs, sit down, or even stand up! It's connected to your hips and thighs and the bones surrounding it. So the next time you have a seat, thank your lucky butt!

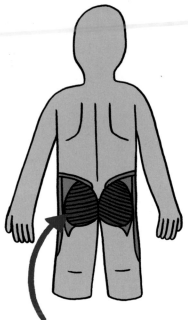

Gluteus maximus

THANKS BUTT!

Does the word "buttocks" make you imagine your butt dressed up in its own tuxedo? Well, try these other butt nicknames on for size!

★ Backside: Butt that's safe for school

★ Behind: Too-obvious butt

★ Bottom: Boring butt

★ Bum: Silly butt

★ Trunk: What's-in-your-butt butt

★ Derrière: Formal butt

★ Tush: Cute-as-a-button butt

★ Fanny: Butt on the run!

★ Hiney: Safe *and* funny—a win-win!

★ Keister: What your silly great-uncle calls the butt

★ Seat: Nobody calls it this

★ Gluteus maximus: Scientific butt (or gladiator butt!)

★ Haunches: *Huh?* Try it out and get back to us.

★ Hindquarters: What they probably called butts in the eighteenth century

★ Posterior: When you're showing off *all* the manners, pop out the ol' "posterior" word and really wow the grownups.

What do *you* call *your* butt?

What in the Wow?

★ Your butt crack has another name . . . a scientific name. Introducing . . . the intergluteal cleft. Drop this term into casual conversations to really wow your friends and family!

Intergluteal cleft (aka butt crack)

★ In the 1880s, during the Victorian era, women often wore *bustles*, or cushions of wire, mesh, and steel, under their dresses to create the appearance of an exaggerated butt.

Wire bustle ➤

Animals Have Butts Too!

Some turtles breathe out of their butts. The Australian Fitzroy River turtle, the North American eastern painted turtle, and the Australian white-throated snapping turtle all breathe through their butts. The endangered Australian white-throated snapping turtle, AKA the "bum-breathing turtle," is able to get nearly 70 percent of its oxygen through its *butt!*

While most two- and four-legged mammals *do* have butts like ours, here is a list of a few animals that do *not*. (Note: if you meet any of these animals, don't bring it up.)

SOME ANIMALS DON'T HAVE BUTTS

Snakes

Dolphins

Giant squids

Alligators

Lobsters

Blue whales

Now close your eyes and imagine your butt on a snake, or a lobster, or any of these animals! And NO LAUGHING!

Buttzville, New Jersey, is a place that exists. It's pretty small, but we just thought it would be nice for you to know that you can choose to live there someday. BUTTZVILLE, USA!

✷ A THANK-YOU LETTER ✷ TO YOUR BODY

Get a partner to serve as either the READER or the WRITER of this letter and grab a blank sheet of paper and a pencil. The WRITER will write the numbers 1–22 on the paper, leaving space for words next to each number. The READER will ask the WRITER for the words needed in the letter and the WRITER will write them down next to the corresponding number. Once completed, the READER will read the full letter to the WRITER, using the WRITER's chosen words. And NO LAUGHING! This is a HEARTFELT LETTER!

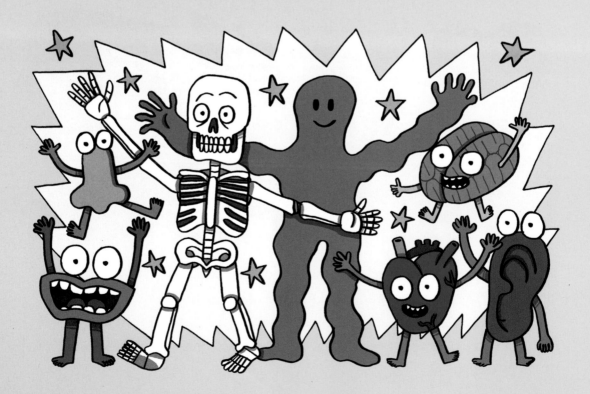

Dear _____ Body,
     1. ADJECTIVE

We've been together a while now— _____ to be exact—and I don't think
                                           2. LENGTH OF TIME

I've ever properly thanked you for all you've done for me. It's because of you that

I'm able to _____ over _____, _____ on _____, and
       3. VERB   4. PLURAL NOUN   5. VERB   6. PLURAL NOUN

_____ through _____. And while it would be difficult for me to
 7. VERB   8. PLURAL NOUN

choose a favorite body part, my _____ has always been something I've been
                                  9. BODY PART

proud to display. It's _____ and famous for its reliability.
              10. ADJECTIVE

    With that said, if I could make one improvement, it would be the ability

to grow an extra _____. A _____, _____, _____,
           11. BODY PART   12. ADJECTIVE 13. ADJECTIVE 14. ADJECTIVE

_____. If I had an extra _____, all my friends would say
  REPEAT 11   REPEAT 11

_____. That would make me so _____.
15. SOMETHING A GROWNUP LIKES TO YELL   16. FEELING

    Finally, I just want you to know that I will promise to take care of you if you

will promise to take care of me. And I will do this by _____
                                          17. SOMETHING YOU DO TO WASTE TIME

and _____.
18. SOMETHING THAT ANNOYS YOUR GROWNUPS

    So thank you, Body. Without you, I'd just be one big _____ _____.
                                          19. ADJECTIVE 20. FAVORITE FOOD

_____ + love,
21. PLURAL NOUN

_____
    22. YOUR FIRST NAME BUT REPLACE
      ALL VOWELS WITH "OODLE"

GLOSSARY

Abdomen—the middle part of your body; your belly.

Allergens—things that aren't actually bad for you but that your body *thinks* are bad and can react strongly to.

Amylase—a type of enzyme that turns starch into sugars that your body uses as energy.

Antivirus—bad guy–buster, like your favorite superhero.

Armpit—the part of your body underneath your shoulder. Oh, who are we kidding?! You know what an armpit is!

Arteries—tubes that transport blood from the heart to other body parts.

Atrium—one of the top cavities of your heart that passes blood up to the lungs and then down to the ventricles.

Bacteria—germs that are so tiny, they only consist of a single cell. Most of them don't hurt you, but some can make you sick.

Bronchioles—small branches in your lungs that lead to air sacs.

Bronchus—the main airway in each lung.

Capillaries—teeny-tiny blood vessels that bring oxygen from your blood to your muscles.

Carbon dioxide—the gas that you breathe (and toot) out, which your body produces from the oxygen that you breathe in.

Cartilage—a firm and flexible padding that covers some parts of your body, like the ends of your nose and the tops of your ears.

Clavicle—the bone that joins your shoulder blades to your sternum.

Collagen—a protein that holds your bones, muscles, and skin together.

Constipation—a condition in which you don't poop as often as you normally do and it becomes difficult to poop.

Dehydration—what happens when you don't drink enough water.

Diarrhea—watery poop that your body makes when it wants to get rid of something it thinks might be making you sick. It's important to drink a lot of water if you have diarrhea, because it can make you dehydrated.

Dust mites—tiny and usually harmless creatures that live on your skin and munch on your dead skin cells.

Eardrum—a thin sheet that separates your ear canal from your middle ear.

Embryo—the first nine weeks of a developing human life.

Enzyme—a kind of protein that helps your body do important things like break down food.

Femur—the upper bone of your leg that supports your weight and lets you walk around.

Fertilization—a process in which two parents provide genes to their offspring (babies).

Freckles—small, brownish spots that cover your skin, often in places that are exposed to the sun.

Gene—a packet of information that contains the instructions for making you into *you*.

Glands—organs that release substances like tears, earwax, or sweat.

Goose bumps—bumps that form automatically at the base of your hairs when you're chilly or scared.

Gums—the soft pink tissue in your mouth that is connected to your teeth and jawbone.

Heart—the super muscular organ in the center of your chest that helps your blood get where it needs to go.

Hormones—chemicals in your body that tell cells and body parts to do certain things— like grow!

Immune system—your body's system to fight against infections.

Large intestine—also known as your colon. These are the larger tubes that food travels to after the small intestine, where what's left of food is drained of water and turned into poop.

Marrow—a soft, fatty substance in the middle of your bones.

Microbes—living things smaller than the human eye can see. Bacteria and viruses are both types of microbes.

Mucosa—the pink, soft tissue that makes up the inside of your mouth and the bottom of your tongue.

Mucus—a slimy substance that keeps parts of your body wet.

Muscles—parts of your body you can stretch and pull to move around.

Nerve cell—a messenger that carries information to and from (and within) the brain.

Olfactory system—the process and organs your body uses to smell.

Organ—a body part that does a job that only it can do to help you stay alive. For example, your lungs are organs that help you breathe.

Platelets—tiny discs that come together to form clots when you start bleeding.

Reproductive system—the organs of the body that are involved in producing babies.

Saliva—spit, the liquid that your mouth makes to keep itself wet.

Salivate—when your mouth becomes wet with saliva after you see or smell a food you enjoy.

Skeleton—the structure of bones that make up your body.

Skull—the bones that form your head and cover the brain.

Small intestine—the tubes in between your stomach and large intestine where most of the nutrients from food get absorbed.

Soft palate—the back of the roof of your mouth.

Spine—your backbone.

Sternum—a long, flat bone in the center of your chest that forms the front part of your rib cage.

Stomach acid—a fluid in your stomach that helps break down food.

Sunburn—red, painful, and irritated skin caused by staying in the sun too long without sunscreen.

Toxin—a material that is dangerous to people or animals and can cause problems if you touch or eat it.

Transplant—the process of taking a part from one person's body and using it in another person's body.

Umbilical cord—a flexible cord that attached you to your birth mother when you were still growing inside her.

Uterus—the female organ in which a baby develops until it's born. Also known as a "womb."

Valves—one-way streets that blood can travel down (but not up).

Veins—tubes that transport blood from your body back to the heart.

Ventricle—one of the bottom cavities of your heart that passes blood to vessels that travel around your body.

Vessels—the highway system that carries your blood through your body.

Virus—a germ that needs a living thing like you to grow and make more of itself. It can make you sick with a cold or the flu.

White blood cells—fighters that help your body get rid of infections and other diseases.

BIBLIOGRAPHY AND RECOMMENDED READING

Books

Macaulay, David. *The Way We Work: Getting to Know the Amazing Human Body*. Boston: Houghton Mifflin Company, 2008.

Natterson, Cara. *Guy Stuff: The Body Book for Boys.* Middleton, WI: American Girl Publishing, 2017.

Schaefer, Valorie Lee. *The Care and Keeping of You 1: The Body Book for Younger Girls*. Rev. ed. Middleton, WI: American Girl Publishing, 2012.

Smithsonian. *Human Body! Your Amazing Body as You've Never Seen It Before*. New York: DK Publishing, 2017.

Weird but True! Human Body. Washington, DC: National Geographic Books, 2017.

Wicks, Maris. *Human Body Theater*. New York: First Second, 2015.

Websites

KidsHealth: kidshealth.org/kid

RECOMMENDED LISTENING

Have your grownup scan the QR code to listen to each episode of *Wow in the World*!

**Laughter in a Can:
How Our Brains
Interpret Funny Business**

**Do You SEE What I
HEAR? The Synesthesia
of Scrambled Senses!**

**G-Force vs. Wasabi:
How the Brain
Registers Pain**

**How to Sleep Your
Way to Victory!**

**Brain
Freeze!**

**Oh Knuck Crackers:
The Science of Poppin'
Knuckles**

**Spit-Take! The Science
of Saliva and Those
Bitter Bites**

**An Eyebrow
Evolution!**

**Getting Nosey About
the Science of Smell:
Why Different Sniffs Get
Different Whiffs!**

SOURCE NOTES

Part I. The Head: Let's Start at the Top
Eyes: The One-Way Windows of the Face

These slimy Ping-Pong balls: Eye Institute, "About Eyes" (www.eyeinstitute.co.nz/about-eyes, August 8, 2019).

Eye muscles that move: NPR, "Looking at What the Eyes See," February 25, 2011 (www.npr.org/2011/02/25/134059275/looking-at-what-the-eyes-see, August 8, 2019).

Could this be because: Donald E. Brown, "Human Universals and Human Culture," Human Behavior & Evolution Society of Japan, November 2003 (www.hbesj.org/HBES-J2003/HumanUniv.pdf, August 9, 2019).

Due to our lack of: Center for Academic Research & Training in Anthropogeny, "Eyebrows" (https://carta.anthropogeny.org/moca/topics/eyebrows, August 9, 2019).

Turns out our brains: Tamami Nakano et al., "Blink-Related Momentary Activation of the Default Mode Network While Viewing Videos," *Proceedings of the National Academy of Sciences* 110, no. 2 (2013): 702–6.

Some babies blink as little: Bahar Gholipour, "Why Do Babies Barely Blink?," Live Science, July 15, 2018 (www.livescience.com/62988-why-babies-rarely-blink.html, August 9, 2019).

Grownups, on the other hand: A. R. Bentivoglio et al., "Analysis of Blink Rate Patterns in Normal Subjects," *Movement Disorders* 12, no. 6 (November 1997): 1028–34 (www.ncbi.nlm.nih.gov/pubmed/9399231, August 9, 2019).

People with blue eyes: University of Copenhagen, "Blue-Eyed Humans Have a Single, Common Ancestor," Science Daily, January 31, 2008 (www.sciencedaily.com/releases/2008/01/080130170343.htm, August 12, 2019).

Some people have: University of Arizona Health Sciences, "Blatt Distichiasis," Hereditary Ocular Disease (https://disorders.eyes.arizona.edu/handouts/blatt-distichiasis, August 12, 2019).

Actress Elizabeth Taylor: Louis Bayard, "Violet Eyes to Die For," *Washington Post*, September 3, 2006 (www.washingtonpost.com/wp-dyn/content/article/2006/08/31/AR2006083101166.html, August 9, 2019).

When you get snotty: KidsHealth, "Why Does My Nose Run?" (www.kidshealth.org/en/kids/nose-run.html, August 12, 2019).

Astronauts cannot cry: Chris Hadfield, "Tears in Space (Don't Fall)" (https://chrishadfield.ca/videos/tears-in-space-dont-fall, August 12, 2019).

People with Heterochromia: David Turbert, "Heterochromia," American Academy of Ophthalmology, February 3, 2017 (www.aao.org/eye-health/diseases/what-is-heterochromia, July 28, 2020).

If unprotected: Moran Eye Center, "Can Your Eyes Get Sunburned?," University of Utah Health, June 22, 2015 (https://healthcare.utah.edu/healthfeed/postings/2015/06/062215_sunburn.eyes.php, August 9, 2019).

In 2007, Kim Goodman: Guinness World Records, "Farthest Eyeball Pop" (www.guinnessworldrecords.com/world-records/23632-farthest-eyeball-pop, August 9, 2019).

Over half of the people: Reena Mukamal, "Why Are Brown Eyes Most Common?," American Academy of Ophthalmology, April 7, 2017 (www.aao.org/eye-health/tips-prevention/why-are-brown-eyes-most-common, August 12, 2019).

Surgeons are unable: David Turbert, "What Parts of the Eye Can Be Transplanted?," American Academy of Ophthalmology, April 3, 2018 (www.aao.org/eye-health/treatments/transplantation-eye, August 9, 2019).

Nose: Let's Get Nosey

On March 18, 2010: Guinness World Records Limited, "Longest Nose on a Living Person," March 18, 2010 (www.guinnessworldrecords.com/world-records/longest-nose-on-a-living-person, July 6, 2019).

GET YOUR GERMY FINGER: J. Thaj and F. Vaz, "Recognising Ear, Nose and Throat Conditions in the Dentist's Chair," *Primary Dental Journal* 6, no. 3 (2017): 39–43.

Boogers contain cavity-fighting: Erica Shapiro Frenkel and Katharina Ribbeck, "Salivary Mucins Protect Surfaces from Colonization by Cariogenic Bacteria," *Applied and Environmental Microbiology*, October 24, 2014 (https://aem.asm.org/content/81/1/332, July 6, 2019).

One small study: J. W. Jefferson and T. D. Thompson, "Rhinotillexomania: Psychiatric Disorder or Habit?," *Journal of Clinical Psychiatry* 56, no. 2 (February 1995): 56–59.

Ears: Hear Ye, Hear Ye!

A single gene in: John H. McDonald, *Myths of Human Genetics* (Baltimore: Sparky House Publishing, 2011), 41–43.

Kids have wetter: Ask Dr. Universe, "Earwax: Why Do We Have It?," April 4, 2016 (askdruniverse.wsu.edu/2016/04/04/earwax-why-do-we-have-it, January 7, 2020).

In 2007, Anthony Victor: Guinness World Records, "Longest Ear Hair" (www.guinnessworldrecords.com/world-records/longest-ear-hair, January 7, 2020).

There's a condition known as: L. Carluer, C. Schupp, and G. L. Defer, "Ear Dyskinesia," *Journal of Neurology, Neurosurgery, and Psychiatry* 77, no. 6 (2006): 802–3.

Mouth: The Biggest Hole in the Human Head

Alligators will regrow: Ping Wu et al., "Specialized Stem Cell Niche Enables Repetitive Renewal of Alligator Teeth," *Proceedings of the National Academy of Sciences of the United States of America* 110, no. 22 (May 28, 2013): E2009–E2018 (www.pnas.org/content/110/22/E2009?with-ds=yes, October 12, 2019).

And over a billion at any one time?: University of Illinois at Chicago College of Dentistry, "The True Story of Why You Get Cavities, According to a Billion Microbes," March 29, 2017 (www.dentistry.uic.edu/patients/cavity-prevention-bacteria, October 12, 2019).

The next time you bust your grandparents: R. Kort et al., "Shaping the Oral Microbiota through Intimate Kissing," *Microbiome* 2, no. 41 (2014) (https://microbiomejournal.biomedcentral.com/articles/10.1186/2049-2618-2-41, October 12, 2019).

Your body makes: Northern Dental Centre, "Fun Facts About Saliva" (www.northerndentalcentre.ca/fun-facts-about-saliva, October 10, 2019).

Pad kid poured: Meera Dolasia, "MIT Researchers Reveal the World's Toughest Tongue Twister!," *Dogo News* (www.dogonews.com/2013/12/7/mit-researchers-reveal-the-worlds-toughest-tongue-twister, October 12, 2019).

Only 10 percent of: Hélène Buithieu, Yves Létourneau, and Rénald Pérusse "Oral Manifestations of Ehlers-Danlos Syndrome," *Journal of the Canadian Dental Association* 67, no. 6 (2001): 330–31.

For centuries, the people: Julia M. White, "Tibet in the 1930s: Theos Bernard's Legacy at UC Berkeley," *Cross Currents e-Journal,* no. 13 (Dec. 2014) (www.cross-currents.berkeley.edu/e-journal/issue-13/Bernard/photo/tibetan-greeting, October 12, 2019).

Ashish Peri, of: Guinness World Records, "Most Tongue to Nose Touches in One Minute" (www.guinnessworldrecords.com/world-records/435650-most-times-touching-your-tongue-to-your-nose-in-one-minute, October 9, 2019).

Thomas Blackstone once: Guinness World Records, "Heaviest Weight Lifted by Tongue" (www.guinnessworldrecords.com/world-records/heaviest-weight-lifted-by-tongue, October 9, 2019).

Blue whales: Michelle Bryner, "What's the Biggest Animal in the World?," Live Science, August 23, 2010 (www.livescience.com/32780-whats-the-biggest-animal-in-the-world.html, October 9, 2019).

In fact, your body: Sandy A. Simon and Ivan E. Araujo, "The Salty and Burning Taste of Capsaicin," *Journal of General Physiology* 125, no. 6 (2005): 531–34.

Part II. The Brain: It's What Makes Up Your Mind!

The brain is mission control: Larissa Hirsch, "Your Brain & Nervous System," Kids Health from Nemours, May 2019 (www.kidshealth.org/en/kids/brain.html, November 2, 2019).

It's powerful: University of Pittsburgh School of Medicine, "About the Brain and Spinal Cord" (www.neurosurgery.pitt.edu/centers/neurosurgical-oncology/brain-and-brain-tumors/about, November 2, 2019).

The brain contains billions: F. A. Azevedo et al., "Equal Numbers of Neuronal and Nonneuronal Cells Make the Human Brain an Isometrically Scaled-Up Primate Brain," *Journal of Comparative Neurology* 513, no. 5 (2009): 532–41.

It gets pretty complicated: David T. Bundy, Nicholas Szrama, Mrinal Pahwa, and Eric C. Leuthardt, "Unilateral, 3D Arm Movement Kinematics Are Encoded in Ipsilateral Human Cortex," *Journal of Neuroscience* 38, no. 47 (2018): 10042–46; Eric H. Chudler, "One Brain . . . Or Two?" University of Washington (www.faculty.washington.edu/chudler/split.html, November 3, 2019).

Cerebrum: Larissa Hirsch, "Your Brain & Nervous System," KidsHealth from Nemours, May 2019 (www.kidshealth.org/en/kids/brain.html, November 2, 2019).

Hypothalamus: Larissa Hirsch, "Your Brain & Nervous System," KidsHealth from Nemours, May 2019 (www.kidshealth.org/en/kids/brain.html, November 2, 2019).

Eat, drink, sleep, repeat: Joseph Proietto, "Chemical Messengers: How Hormones Make Us Feel Hungry and Full," The Conversation, September 25, 2015 (www.theconversation.com/chemical-messengers-how-hormones-make-us-feel-hungry-and-full-35545, November 5, 2019).

We keep track of: R. Szymusiak and D. McGinty, "Hypothalamic Regulation of Sleep and Arousal," *Annals of the New York Academy of Sciences* 1129 (2008): 275–86.

Pituitary Gland: Larissa Hirsch, "Your Brain & Nervous System," KidsHealth from Nemours, May 2019 (www.kidshealth.org/en/kids/brain.html, November 2, 2019).

Come visit if you're in search of: Stanford Children's Health, "Anatomy of a Child's Brain" (www.stanfordchildrens.org/en/topic/default?id=anatomy-of-a-childs-brain-90-P02588, November 2, 2019).

Brain Stem: Larissa Hirsch, "Your Brain & Nervous System," KidsHealth from Nemours, May 2019 (www.kidshealth.org/en/kids/brain.html, November 2, 2019).

Spinal Cord: Stanford Children's Health, "Anatomy of a Child's Brain" (www.stanfordchildrens.org/en/topic/default?id=anatomy-of-a-childs-brain-90-P02588, November 2, 2019).

Amygdala: Larissa Hirsch, "Your Brain & Nervous System," KidsHealth from Nemours, May 2019 (www.kidshealth.org/en/kids/brain.html, November 2, 2019).

Mostly because I process light: Eric H. Chudler, "Lobes of the Brain," University of Washington (www.faculty.washington.edu/chudler/split.html, November 3, 2019).

I'm good at: Eric H. Chudler, "Lobes of the Brain," University of Washington (www.faculty.washington.edu/chudler/split.html, November 3, 2019).

The average adult brain: National Institute of Neurological Disorders and Stroke, "Brain Basics: Know Your Brain" (www.ninds.nih.gov/Disorders/Patient-Caregiver-Education/Know-Your-Brain, November 5, 2019).

A newborn baby's brain: Bahar Gholipour, "Babies' Amazing Brain Growth Revealed in New Map," Live Science, August 11, 2014 (www.livescience.com/47298-babies-amazing-brain-growth.html, November 5, 2019).

The human brain is: John H. Kaas, "The Evolution of Brains from Early Mammals to Humans," *Wiley Interdisciplinary Review of Cognitive Science* 4, no. 1 (2013): 33–35.

By the time you turn nine: V. S. Caviness Jr. et al., "The Human Brain Age 7–11 Years: A Volumetric Analysis Based on Magnetic Resonance Images," *Cerebral Cortex* 6, no. 5 (1996): 726–36.

While your brain only: Eric H. Chudler, "Brain Facts That Make You Go Hmmm," University of Washington (www.faculty.washington.edu/chudler/split.html, November 3, 2019).

It uses 20 percent: Ferris Jabr, "Does Thinking Hard Really Burn More Calories?" *Scientific American*, July 18, 2012 (www.scientificamerican.com/article/thinking-hard-calories, November 3, 2019).

The brain can store: Paul Reber, "What Is the Memory Capacity of the Human Brain?," *Scientific American*, May 1, 2010 (www.scientificamerican.com/article/what-is-the-memory-capacity, November 5, 2019).

The human brain is as big as the whole internet: Thomas M. Bartol Jr. et al., "Nanoconnectomic Upper Bound on the Variability of Synaptic Plasticity," eLife Sciences, November 30, 2015 (www.elifesciences.org/articles/10778, November 3, 2019).

It's limited by how quickly: Patrick Monahan, "The Human Brain Is as Big as the Internet," American Association for the Advancement of Science, January 25, 2016 (www.sciencemag.org/news/2016/01/human-brain-big-internet, November 4, 2019).

You have at least one thousand: Carl Zimmer, "100 Trillion Connections: New Efforts Probe and Map the Brain's Detailed Architecture," *Scientific American*, January 2011 (www.scientificamerican.com/article/100-trillion-connections, November 4, 2019).

A neural connection: Valerie Ross, "Numbers: The Nervous System, From 268-MPH Signals to Trillions of Synapses," *Discover Magazine*, May 14, 2011 (www.discovermagazine.com/health/numbers-the-nervous-system-from-268-mph-signals-to-trillions-of-synapses, November 4, 2019).

Pain signals: Tim Welsh, "It Feels Instantaneous, But How Long Does It Really Take to Think a Thought?," The Conversation, June 26, 2015 (theconversation.com/it-feels-instantaneous-but-how-long-does-it-really-take-to-think-a-thought-42392, November 5, 2019).

During rest, your brain is: Erin J. Wamsley and Robert Stickgold, "Memory, Sleep and Dreaming: Experiencing Consolidation," *Sleep Medicine Clinics Journal* 6, no. 1 (2011): 97–108.

A 2015 study: Jessica Hamzelou, "Ultra-marathon Runners' Brains Shrank While Racing across Europe," *New Scientist*, December 2, 2015 (www.newscientist.com/article/dn28591-ultra-marathon-runners-brains-shrunk-while-racing-across-europe, November 5, 2019).

The good news is: Wolfgang Freund et al., "Regionally Accentuated Reversible Brain Grey Matter Reduction in Ultra Marathon Runners Detected by Voxel-Based Morphometry," *BMC Sports Science, Medicine, and Rehabilitation* 6, no. 1 (2014): 4.

If you could smooth out: Rachel Nuwer, "Why Are Our Brains Wrinkly?" *Smithsonian Magazine*, February 28, 2013 (www.smithsonianmag.com/smart-news/why-are-our-brains-wrinkly-29271143, November 5, 2019).

It would flatten out: Roberto Toro, "On the Possible Shapes of the Brain," *Evolutionary Biology* 39 (2012): 600–612.

Part III. From the Outside In
Skin: It's What Keeps Your Insides In!

It weighs about as much: Eric H. Chudler, "Brain Facts That Make You Go Hmmm," University of Washington (www.faculty.washington.edu/chudler/split.html, November 3, 2019).

Skin is your fastest: American Academy of Dermatology Association, "What Kids Should Know about the Layers of Skin" (www.aad.org/public/parents-kids/healthy-habits/parents/kids/skin-layers, August 5, 2019).

If we were to save up: Kids Health from Nemours, "Your Skin" (www.kidshealth.org/en/kids/skin.html, August 5, 2019).

Dust mite mouths: Claire Landsbaum, "How Gross Is Your Mattress?" Slate, November 24, 2015 (www.slate.com/human-interest/2015/11/mattresses-dust-mites-and-skin-cells-how-gross-does-your-mattress-get-over-time.html, August 2, 2019).

The thickest skin: Act for Libraries, "The Thickest and Thinnest Skin in the Body" (www.actforlibraries.org/the-thickest-and-thinnest-skin-in-the-body, August 5, 2019).

In 1999, Gary Turner: Guinness World Records, "Stretchiest Skin" (www.guinnessworldrecords.com/world-records/72387-stretchiest-skin, August 5, 2019).

Pimples, AKA Zits: American Academy of Dermatology Association, "What Is Acne?" (www.aad.org/public/parents-kids/lesson-plans/lesson-plan-what-is-acne-ages-8-10, August 5, 2019).

Moles! What are they?: American Academy of Dermatology Association, "Moles: Who Gets and Types" (www.aad.org/public/diseases/a-z/moles-types, August 5, 2019).

Eczema, AKA Dermatitis: American Academy of Dermatology Association, "Eczema Resource Center" (www.aad.org/public/diseases/eczema, August 5, 2019).

Birthmarks!: American Academy of Dermatology Association. "What Kids Should Know about Birthmarks" (www.aad.org/public/parents-kids/healthy-habits/parents/kids/birthmarks-kids, August 5, 2019).

Sweat: Eww! What's That Smell?

These hungry microbes: Jessica Boddy, "Your Body Means the World to the Microbes That Live On It," *Popular Science*, August 24, 2018 (www.popsci.com/microbes-on-your-body, August 5, 2019).

Meat sweats: Brandon Specktor, "The Truth About 'Meat Sweats,' According to Science," Live Science, June 27, 2018 (www.livescience.com/62932-meat-sweats-causes.html, August 6, 2019).

Nails: Nailed It!

Nails grow: New York Times "Q & A," August 2, 1988 (www.nytimes.com/1988/08/02/science/q-a-504688.html, August 6, 2019).

Kids' fingernails grow: Donna M. D'Alessandro, "How Fast Do Fingernails Grow?," Pediatric Education.org, November 5, 2012 (www.pediatriceducation.org/2012/11/05/how-fast-do-fingernails-grow, August 6, 2019).

Nails grow faster: New York Times, "Q & A," August 2, 1988 (www.nytimes.com/1988/08/02/science/q-a-504688.html, August 6, 2019).

Nails are as strong: New Scientist, "Fingernails Have the Strength of Hooves," February 7, 2004 (www.newscientist.com/article/mg18124332-600-fingernails-have-the-strength-of-hooves, August 7, 2019).

If you lose a fingernail: American Academy of Dermatology Association, "What Kids Should Know About How Nails Grow" (www.aad.org/public/parents-kids/healthy-habits/parents/kids/nails-grow, August 6, 2019).

About half of kids: Nationwide Children's Hospital, "Nail Biting Prevention and Habit Reversal Tips: How to Get Your Child to Stop," January 11, 2019 (www.nationwidechildrens.org/family-resources-education/700childrens/2018/01/nail-biting-prevention-and-habit-reversal-tips-how-to-get-your-child-to-stop, August 7, 2019).

But in 2018, at the age: David Stubbings, "Owner of World's Longest Nails Has Them Cut after Growing Them for 66 Years," Guinness World Records, July 11, 2018 (www. guinnessworldrecords.com/news/2018/7/owner-of-worlds-longest-nails-has-them-cut-after-growing-them-for-66-years-532563, August 7, 2019).

Hair: The Long and Short of It

We've got follicles big: Francisco Jimenez, Ander Izeta, and Enrique Poblet, "Morphometric Analysis of the Human Scalp Hair Follicle: Practical Implications for the Hair Transplant Surgeon and Hair Regeneration Studies," *Dermatologic Surgery* 37, no. 1 (2011): 58–64.

Choose a specific shape: Sebastien Thibaut, Philippe Barbarat, Frederic Leroy, and Bruno A. Bernard, "Human Hair Keratin Network and Curvature," *International Journal of Dermatology* 46, no. s1 (2007): 7–10.

"For fabulous coils and curls": Leidamarie Tirado-Lee, "The Science of Curls," Science in Society of Northwestern University, May 20, 2014. (helix.northwestern.edu/blog/2014/05/science-curls, January 5, 2020).

Customers can expect: Morgan B. Murphrey, Sanjay Agarwal, and Patrick M. Zito, "Anatomy, Hair" (Treasure Island, FL: StatPearls Publishing, 2019; www.ncbi.nlm.nih.gov/books/NBK513312, January 5, 2020).

Vellus hair and terminal hair: Ezra Hoover, Mandy Alhajj, and Jose L. Flores, "Physiology, Hair" (Treasure Island, FL: StatPearls Publishing, 2019; www.ncbi.nlm.nih.gov/books/NBK499948, January 5, 2020).

Teenagers and grownups: Dahlia Saleh and Christopher Cook, "Hypertrichosis" (Treasure Island, FL: StatPearls Publishing, 2019; www.pubmed.ncbi.nlm.nih.gov/30521275-hypertrichosis, January 5, 2020).

Where you WON'T find hair: Ezra Hoover, Mandy Alhajj, and Jose L. Flores, "Physiology, Hair" (Treasure Island, FL: StatPearls Publishing, 2019; www.ncbi.nlm.nih.gov/books/NBK499948, January 5, 2020).

These are all examples of: R. Kumar et al., "Glabrous Lesional Stem Cells Differentiated into Functional Melanocytes: New Hope for Repigmentation," *Journal of the European Academy of Dermatology and Venereology* 30, no. 9 (2016): 1555–60.

Part IV. How We Move
Bones: There Is a Skeleton Living Inside You!

Most fragile: Lincoln Orthopaedic Center, "Most Commonly Broken Bones" (www.ortholinc.com/article-id-fix/272-most-commonly-broken-bones, August 9, 2019).

The stapes is also the smallest: Bradley L. Njaa, *Pathological Basis of Veterinary Disease* (Maryland Heights: Mosby, 2017).

The femur, also the longest: Healthline, "Femur," April 2, 2015 (www.healthline.com/human-body-maps/femur#1, August 10, 2019).

Every bone in your body is connected: Bradley J. Fikes, "Body Parts: The Hyoid—A Little Known Bone," *Hartford Courant,* March 11, 2007 (www.courant.com/sdut-body-parts-the-hyoid-a-little-known-bone-2007mar11-story.html, July 24, 2020).

Some of your bones are able: Karl J. Jepsen, "Systems Analysis of Bone," *Wiley Interdisciplinary Reviews, Systems Biology and Medicine* 1, no. 1 (2009): 73–88.

Most people have twenty-four: Michael Hinck, "Did You Know—One out of Every 200 People Are Born with an Extra Rib?," Flushing Hospital Medical Center, April 20, 2018 (www.flushinghospital.org/newsletter/did-you-know-one-out-of-every-200-people-are-born-with-an-extra-rib, August 14, 2019).

More than half. S. G. Uppin et al., "Lesions of the Bones of the Hands and Feet: A Study of 50 Cases," *Archives of Pathology and Laboratory Medicine* 132, no. 5 (2008): 800–812.

Muscles: Turning Your Body into a Tyrannosaurus FLEX!

Skeletal muscle: Library of Congress, "What Is the Strongest Muscle in the Human Body?" (www.loc.gov/everyday-mysteries/item/what-is-the-strongest-muscle-in-the-human-body, August 12, 2019).

Ancient Romans thought: Online Etymology Dictionary, "Muscle" (www.etymonline.com/word/muscle, August 12, 2019).

A grownup's body weight is: Ian Janssen, Steven B. Heymsfield, ZiMian Wang, and Robert Ross, "Skeletal Muscle Mass and Distribution in 468 Men and Women aged 18–88 yr," *Journal of Applied Physiology* 89, no. 1 (2000): 81–88.

You have more than six hundred: Kids Health from Nemours, "Your Muscles" (www.kidshealth.org/en/kids/muscles.html, August 1, 2019).

Your eye muscles: Talk of the Nation, "Looking at What the Eyes See," NPR, February 23, 2011 (www.npr.org/2011/02/25/134059275/looking-at-what-the-eyes-see, August 2, 2019).

Every single one of the five million: "How to Be Human: The Reason We Are So Scarily Hairy," *New Scientist*, October 4, 2017 (www.newscientist.com/article/mg23631460-700-why-are-humans-so-hairy, August 5, 2019).

Has its own muscle: Niloufar Torkamani, Nicholas W. Rufaut, Leslie Jones, and Rodney D. Sinclair. "Beyond Goosebumps: Does the Arrector Pili Muscle Have a Role in Hair Loss?," *International Journal of Trichology* 6, no. 3 (2014): 88–94

Put your hands together for: A. J. Harris et al., "Muscle Fiber and Motor Unit Behavior in the Longest Human Skeletal Muscle," *Journal of Neuroscience* 25, no. 37 (2005): 8528–33.

It's the GLUTEUS MAXIMUS: Library of Congress, "What Is the Strongest Muscle in the Human Body?" (www.loc.gov/everyday-mysteries/item/what-is-the-strongest-muscle-in-the-human-body, August 12, 2019).

Let's give a big round of applause for the STAPEDIUS: K. C. Prasad et al., "Microsurgical Anatomy of Stapedius Muscle: Anatomy Revisited, Redefined with Potential Impact in Surgeries," *Indian Journal of Otolaryngology and Head & Neck Surgery* 71, no. 1 (2019): 14–18.

Part V. Pump It Up, Go with the Flow
Heart: It Lubs You!

That's one hundred thousand beats: PBS Nova, "Amazing Heart Facts" (www.pbs.org/wgbh/nova/heart/heartfacts.html, August 20, 2019).

Newborn babies: Stanford Children's Health, "Assessments of Newborn Babies" (www.stanfordchildrens.org/en/topic/default?id=assessments-for-newborn-babies-90-P02336, August 20, 2019).

Kids: Bahar Gholipour, "What Is a Normal Heart Rate?" Live Science, January 12, 2018 (www.livescience.com/42081-normal-heart-rate.html, August 10, 2019).

Adults: Harvard Health Publishing, "What Your Heart Rate Is Telling You," October 23, 2018. (www.health.harvard.edu/heart-health/what-your-heart-rate-is-telling-you, August 20, 2019).

Like a whole cup of blood: Healthwise, "Cardiac Output," July 22, 2018 (uofmhealth.org/health-library/tx4080abcm, August 20, 2019).

A kid's heart is: Garyfalia Ampanozia et al., "Comparing Fist Size to Heart Size Is Not a Viable Technique to Assess Cardiomegaly," *Cardiovascular Pathology* 36 (2018): 1–5

Your heart is powered by: Johns Hopkins Medicine, "Anatomy and Function of the Heart's Electrical System" (www.hopkinsmedicine.org/health/conditions-and-diseases/anatomy-and-function-of-the-hearts-electrical-system, August 10, 2019).

The average adult man's heart weighs: D. Kimberley Molina and Vincent J. M. DiMaio, "Normal Organ Weights in Men: Part I—The Heart," *American Journal of Forensic Medical Pathology* 33, no. 4 (2012): 362–67.

When two people in love hold hands: Lisa Marshall, "A Lover's Touch Eases Pain as Heartbeats, Breathing Sync," CU Boulder Today, June 21, 2017 (www.colorado.edu/today/2017/06/21/lovers-touch-eases-pain-heartbeats-breathing-sync, August 10, 2019).

Your heart makes enough energy: Mark Zimmer, *Illuminating Disease: An Introduction to Green Fluorescent Proteins* (New York: Oxford University Press, 2015).

On average, your heart beats: American Heart Association, "About Arrhythmia," September 2016 (www.heart.org/HEARTORG/Conditions/Arrhythmia/AboutArrthmia/About-Arrthmia_UCM_002010_Article.jsp?appName=MobileApp, August 10, 2019).

Blood: Not as Gross When It's Inside Your Body

The RBCs get their brilliant red: US National Library of Medicine, "Circulation Station" (www.cfmedicine.nlm.nih.gov/activities/circulatory_text.html, August 12, 2019).

Life expectancy: Four months: Robert S. Franco, "Measurement of Red Cell Lifespan and Aging," *Transfusion Medicine and Hemotherapy* 39, no. 5 (2012): 302–7.

A whole army of little fighters: "High White Blood Cell Count," Mayo Clinic, November 30, 2018 (www.mayoclinic.org/symptoms/high-white-blood-cell-count/basics/causes/sym-20050611, August 12, 2019).

Life expectancy: A few hours: Jose Borghans and Ruy M Ribeiro, "T-Cell Immunology: The Maths of Memory," *eLife* 6 (2017) (www.elifesciences.org/articles/26754, August 12, 2019).

Controlling the blood: Franklin Institute, "All About Scabs" (www.fi.edu/heart/all-about-scabs, August 10, 2019).

Life expectancy: Ten days: Nicole LeBrasseur, "Platelets' Preset Lifespan," *Journal of Cell Biology* 177, no. 2 (2007): 186.

A newborn baby's body: Miller Children's and Women's Hospital, "Facts about Donating Blood" (www.millerchildrenshospitallb.org/centers-programs/facts-about-donating-blood, August 10, 2019).

The smallest blood vessel: Franklin Institute, "Blood Vessels" (www.fi.edu/heart/blood-vessels, August 1, 2019).

The blood in your body travels: PBS Nova, "Amazing Heart Facts" (www.pbs.org/wgbh/nova/heart/heartfacts.html, August 8, 2019).

Your blood makes up almost 8 percent: American Society of Hematology, "Blood Basics" (www.hematology.org/Patients/Basics, August 10, 2019).

One blood cell goes through the heart: US National Library of Medicine, "Circulation Station" (www.cfmedicine.nlm.nih.gov/activities/circulatory_text.html, August 12, 2019).

Lungs: [More Than] Just a Couple of Ol' Windbags

Actually smaller than I am: Raheel Chaudhry and Bruno Bordoni, "Anatomy, Thorax, Lungs" (Treasure Island, FL: StatPearls Publishing 2019; www.ncbi.nlm.nih.gov/books/NBK470197, January 5, 2020).

And each bronchiole stems: Apeksh Patwa and Amit Shah, "Anatomy and Physiology of Respiratory System Relevant to Anaesthesia," *Indian Journal of Anaesthesia* 59, no. 9 (2015): 533–41.

Covered in a web of: Latent Semantic Analysis at University of Colorado Boulder, "The Role of the Lungs" (www.lsa.colorado.edu/essence/texts/lungs.html, January 5, 2020).

These six hundred million: Matthias Ochs et al., "The Number of Alveoli in the Human Lung," *American Journal of Respiratory and Critical Care Medicine* 169, no. 1 (2004) (https://doi.org/10.1164/rccm.200308-1107OC, April 11, 2020).

18 to 30: The number of breaths: Eleesha Lockett, "What Is a Normal Respiratory Rate for Kids and Adults?," Healthline, March 14, 2019 (www.healthline.com/health/normal-respiratory-rate, January 4, 2020).

More than 2,000 gallons: American Lung Association, "How Your Lungs Get the Job Done," April 11, 2018 (www.lung.org/about-us/blog/2017/07/how-your-lungs-work.html, January 4, 2020).

1,500 miles (2,400 km): American Lung Association, "How Your Lungs Get the Job Done," April 11, 2018 (www.lung.org/about-us/blog/2017/07/how-your-lungs-work.html, January 4, 2020).

600 million: National Geographic "Lungs" (www.nationalgeographic.com/science/health-and-human-body/human-body/lungs/#close, January 6, 2020).

Over 500 million: Jack L. Feldman and Christopher A. Del Negro, "Looking for Inspiration: New Perspectives on Respiratory Rhythm," *Nature Reviews Neuroscience* 7, no. 3 (2006): 232.

Urinary System: Pee-Pee Power!

Our urinary system is made: KidsHealth from Nemours, "Your Urinary System" (www.kidshealth.org/en/kids/pee.html, July 10, 2019).

Kidneys (NOT to Be Confused with "Kid Knees"): Larissa Hirsch, "Your Kidneys," KidsHealth from Nemours, September 2018 (www.kidshealth.org/en/kids/kidneys.html, July 13, 2019).

"Bilateral symmetry": Brooke Huuskes, "Curious Kids: Why Do We Have Two Kidneys When We Can Live with Only One?," The Conversation, March 18, 2019 (www. theconversation.com/curious-kids-why-do-we-have-two-kidneys-when-we-can-live-with-only-one-113201, July 12, 2019).

The bladder acts as a: Michael Huckabee, "Mind over Bladder: To Hold or Not to Hold," University of Nebraska Medical Center, June 5, 2014 (www.unmc.edu/news.cfm?match=15242, July 12, 2019).

It holds roughly one and a half to two cups: National Institute of Diabetes and Digestive and Kidney Diseases, "The Urinary Tract and How It Works," January 2014 (www.niddk.nih.gov/health-information/urologic-diseases/urinary-tract-how-it-works, July 12, 2019).

Asparagus Whiz: Benjamin Franklin, *Fart Proudly* (New York: Penguin Random House, 2003).

May be linked to genetics: Sarah C Markt et al., "Sniffing Out Significant 'Pee Values': Genome Wide Association Study of Asparagus Anosmia," *BMJ* 355, no. i6071 (2016) (www.ncbi.nlm.nih.gov/pmc/articles/PMC5154975, August 10, 2019).

Brush their teeth with pee: Kristina Killgrove, "6 Practical Ways Romans Used Human Urine and Feces in Daily Life," Mental Floss, March 14, 2016 (www.mentalfloss.com/article/76994/6-practical-ways-romans-used-human-urine-and-feces-daily-life, July 20, 2019).

The US Army Manual: U.S Army Field Manual 3-05.70 (Washington, DC: United States Army, 2002) (www.web.archive.org/web/20090612013729/http:/www.equipped.com/21-76/ch6.pdf, July 20, 2019).

People pee between six and seven: Bladder and Bowel Community, "Urinary Frequency" (www.bladderandbowel.org/bladder/bladder-conditions-and-symptoms/frequency, July 20, 2019).

Part VI. Digestion: How to Transform Your Food into Poop!
Digestion: Taking a Ride Down the Digestive Slide

Before food even enters your mouth: Larissa Hirsch, "Digestive System," KidsHealth from Nemours, May 2019 (www. kidshealth.org/en/parents/digestive.html?WT.ac=p-ra, June 2, 2019).

Food doesn't need gravity's help: Larissa Hirsch, "Digestive System," KidsHealth from Nemours, May 2019 (www. kidshealth.org/en/parents/digestive.html?WT.ac=p-ra, June 2, 2019).

The small intestine is about: KidsHealth from Nemours, "Your Digestive System" (www.kidshealth.org/en/kids/digestive-system.html, June 8, 2019).

The large intestine is about: KidsHealth from Nemours, "Your Digestive System" (www.kidshealth.org/en/kids/digestive-system.html, June 8, 2019).

A grownup's entire digestive tract: American Society for Gastrointestinal Endoscopy, "Quick Anatomy Lesson: Human Digestive System," August 2014 (www.asge.org/home/about-asge/newsroom/media-backgrounders-detail/human-digestive-system, June 8, 2019).

Poop: The Scoop on Poop

In 1997, Dr. Ken Heaton: S. J. Lewis and K. W. Heaton, "Stool Form Scale as a Useful Guide to Intestinal Transit Time," *Scandinavian Journal of Gastroenterology* 32, no. 9 (1997): 920–24.

75 percent water and 25 percent: C. Rose, A. Parker, B. Jefferson, and E. Cartmell, "The Characterization of Feces and Urine: A Review of the Literature to Inform Advanced Treatment Technology," *Critical Reviews in Environmental Science and Technology* 45, no. 17 (2015): 1827–79.

According to a 2003 study: Dov Sikirov, "Comparison of Straining During Defecation in Three Positions: Results and Implications for Human Health," *Digestive Diseases and Sciences* 48 (2003): 1201–5.

While we don't know: Ainara Sistiaga, Carolina Mallol, Bertila Galván, and Roger Everett Summons, "The Neanderthal Meal: A New Perspective Using Faecal Biomarkers," *PLOS One* 9, no. 6 (2014) (www.journals.plos.org/plosone/article?id=10.1371/journal.pone.0101045, July 10, 2019).

The Gas Station: Tooting Your Own Horn

The average healthy person: Purna Kashyap, "Why Do We Pass Gas?" TED ED (www.ed.ted.com/lessons/why-do-we-pass-gas-purna-kashyap, July 10, 2019).

The Guinness World Record for Loudest Recorded: Rachel Swatman, "Loudest Burp—Meet the Record Breakers Video," Guinness World Records, April 21, 2016 (www.guinnessworldrecords.com/news/2016/4/loudest-burp-%E2%80%93-meet-the-record-breakers-video-425916?fb_comment_id=1024674550935142_1103725996363330, July 10, 2019).

Part VII. The Immune System: Siiiiick

Every day, microscopic invaders: MedlinePlus, "Immune Response" (www.medlineplus.gov/ency/article/000821.htm, July 10, 2020).

They have the power to multiply: M. Drexler, *What You Need to Know About Infectious Disease* (Washington, DC: National Academies Press, 2010), 23–24.

Release harmful molecules called toxins: James Byrne, "Bacterial Toxins," *Scientific American,* November 10, 2011 (blogs.scientificamerican.com/disease-prone/bacterial-toxins, July 10, 2020).

Most are pretty harmless: Gabriela Jorge Da Silva and Sara Domingues, "We Are Never Alone: Living with the Human Microbiota," *Frontiers for Young Minds,* July 17, 2017 (kids.frontiersin.org/article/10.3389/frym.2017.00035, July 10, 2020).

The kind in your gut: Jo Napolitano, "Exploring the Role of Gut Bacteria in Digestion," Argonne National Laboratory, August 19, 2010 (www.anl.gov/article/exploring-the-role-of-gut-bacteria-in-digestion, July 10, 2020).

They reproduce by invading a body cell: National Geographic Society, "Viruses" (www.nationalgeographic.org/encyclopedia/viruses, July 12, 2020).

Hitching a ride on the food you eat: Centers for Disease Control and Prevention, "Foodborne Germs and Illnesses" (www.cdc.gov/foodsafety/foodborne-germs.html, July 12, 2020).

Disguising themselves in the air you breathe: E. L. Bodie et al., "Urban Aerosols Harbor Diverse and Dynamic Bacterial Populations," *Proceedings of the National Academy of Sciences of the United States of America* 104, no. 1 (2007): 299–304.

Trap germs with its super-stick power: Greta Friar, "Mucus Does More Than You Think," *MIT Scope,* March 17, 2017 (scopeweb.mit.edu/mucus-does-more-than-you-think-8b12f8f6feae, July 12, 2020).

Chemical-filled and ready to kill: T. Vila, A. M. Rizk, et. Al, "The Power of Saliva: Antimicrobial and Beyond," *PLOS Pathogens* 15, no. 11 (2019) (www.doi.org/10.1371/journal.ppat.1008058, July 12, 2020).

You're washing away: Centers for Disease Control and Prevention, "Show Me the Science—Why Wash Your Hands?" (www.cdc.gov/handwashing/why-handwashing.html, July 12, 2020).

Part VIII. The Reproductive System: How Humans Make Humans
The Circle of Life: Let's Explore!

It can heal its own: Reena Mukamal, "How Humans See in Color," American Academy of Ophthalmology, June 8, 2017 (www.aao.org/eye-health/tips-prevention/how-humans-see-in-color, February 2, 2020).

Create a new layer of skin: Kids Health from Nemours, "Your Skin" (www.kidshealth.org/en/kids/skin.html, February 2, 2020).

The male cells are called: Steven Dowshen, "All About Puberty," Kids Health from Nemours, October 2015 (www.kidshealth.org/en/kids/puberty.html, February 4, 2020).

This embryo will grow: Steven Dowshen, "All About Puberty," Kids Health from Nemours, October 2015 (www.kidshealth.org/en/kids/puberty.html, February 4, 2020).

However, sometime between: Steven Dowshen, "All About Puberty," Kids Health from Nemours, October 2015 (www.kidshealth.org/en/kids/puberty.html, February 4, 2020).

Puberty tends to occur: Steven Dowshen, "All About Puberty," Kids Health from Nemours, October 2015 (www.kidshealth.org/en/kids/puberty.html, February 20, 2020).

Puberty: Whaterty?

Expect a rapid growth: Cleveland Clinic, "Boys, BO and Peach Fuzz: What to Expect in Puberty," December 7, 2017 (www.health.clevelandclinic.org/boys-bo-and-peach-fuzz-what-to-expect-in-puberty/, February 4, 2020).

Boys may notice: Cleveland Clinic, "Boys, BO and Peach Fuzz: What to Expect in Puberty," December 7, 2017 (www.health.clevelandclinic.org/boys-bo-and-peach-fuzz-what-to-expect-in-puberty/, February 4, 2020).

Girls may notice: Cleveland Clinic, "Puberty: Is Your Daughter On Track, Ahead Or Behind?" December 28, 2017 (www.health.clevelandclinic.org/puberty-in-girls-whats-normal-and-whats-not/, February 5, 2020).

Everyone can count on: Stanford Children's Health, "Puberty: Teen Girl" (www.stanfordchildrens.org/en/topic/default?id=puberty-adolescent-female-90-P01635, February 5, 2020).

Puberty hormones are: Alicia Diaz-Thomas, Henry Anhalt, and Christine Burt Solorzano, "Puberty," Hormone Health Network, May 2019 (www.hormone.org/diseases-and-conditions/puberty, February 24, 2020).

Pimples or acne are: American Academy of Dermatology Association, "Acne: Who Gets It and Causes" (www.aad.org/public/diseases/acne/causes/acne-causes, February 24, 2020).

During puberty, your: Dominique F. Maciejewski et al., "A 5-Year Longitudinal Study on Mood Variability Across Adolescence Using Daily Diaries," *Child Development* 86, no. 6 (2015): 1908–21.

When it comes time: UCLA Health, "Sleep and Teens" (www.uclahealth.org/sleepcenter/sleep-and-teens, February 16, 2020).

A hormone called melatonin: Kyla Wahlstrom, "Sleepy Teenage Brains Need School to Start Later in the Morning," The Conversation, September 12, 2017 (www.theconversation.com/sleepy-teenage-brains-need-school-to-start-later-in-the-morning-82484, February 17, 2020).

If there's one thing: Steven Dowshen, "All About Puberty," Kids Health from Nemours, October 2015 (www.kidshealth.org/en/kids/puberty.html, February 20, 2020).

During puberty, you might start: Steven Dowshen, "Your Changing Voice," Kids Health from Nemours, October 2015 (www.kidshealth.org/en/kids/puberty.html, February 20, 2020).

There are actually many more ways: Planned Parenthood, "What Is Intersex?" (www.plannedparenthood.org/learn/gender-identity/sex-gender-identity/whats-intersex, March 23, 2020).

Bonus Body: The Butt

"The two round fleshy parts": Lexico, powered by Oxford, "Buttock," Oxford English Dictionary (www.lexico.com/en/definition/buttock, July 27, 2020).

Located underneath a layer of fat: Stephanie Dolgoff, "The Complete Guide to Your Butt Muscles," *Shape,* March 2, 2020 (www.shape.com/fitness/tips/butt-muscles-guide, July 12, 2020).

Largest and most powerful: Lily Norton, "What's the Strongest Muscle in the Human Body?" Live Science, September 29, 2010 (www.livescience.com/32823-strongest-human-muscles.html, July 12, 2020).

Women often wore bustles: Fashion Institute of Technology, "Bustle," Fashion History Timeline, December 27, 2017 (fashionhistory.fitnyc.edu/bustle, July 12, 2020).

Some turtles breathe out of their butts: John R. Platt, "Butt-Breathing Turtle Now Critically Endangered," *Scientific American,* December 12, 2014 (blogs.scientificamerican.com/extinction-countdown/butt-breathing-turtle-now-critically-endangered, July 12, 2020).

70 percent of its oxygen: R. Muryn et al., "Health and Hibernation of Freshwater Turtles," ResearchGate, July 14, 2018 (www.researchgate.net/publication/326400528_Health_and_Hibernation_of_Freshwater_Turtles, July 12, 2020).

Buttzville, New Jersey: Peter Genovese, "From Buttzville to Bivalve: N.J.'s 20 Most Colorfully Named Towns," NJ.com, August 27, 2015 (www.nj.com/entertainment/2015/08/njs_20_most_colorfully-named_towns_miami_beach_man.html, July 12, 2020).

PHOTO CREDITS

7activestudio/iStock/Getty Images: 97 (top)

Scott Barbour/Getty Images: 61

max blain/Shutterstock: 97 (bottom)

Paul Brown/Chronicle/Alamy: 158

C Squared Studios/Photodisc/Getty Images: 113, 132 (top, bottom)

Steve Cole/Photodisc/Getty Images: 34

DuohuaEr/Alamy: 144 (bottom left)

gfrandsen/iStock/Getty Images: 127

Guinness World Records Limited: 14, 16, 26 (top), 37, 71

hideous410grapher/iStock/Getty Images: 26 (bottom left), 144 (bottom right)

Houghton Mifflin Harcourt: 52 (left), 65 (bottom), 106

Guy Jarvis/Houghton Mifflin Harcourt: 52 (right)

©kickers/iStockphoto.com: 11

Dan Kosmayer/Shutterstock: 18

Nick Koudis/Photodisc/Getty Images: 26 (top right, bottom right)

Michael Krinke/iStockphoto.com: 64 (bottom)

RyanJLane/E+/Getty Images: 129

Gang Liu/Shutterstock: 26 (top left)

©ltummy/Shutterstock: 84

PeterTG/iStock/Getty Images: 64 (top)

Ingrid Prats/Shutterstock: 88

Roberts Ratuts/Alamy: 108 (top)

John A. Rizzo/Photodisc/Getty Images: 74

schankz/Shutterstock: 144 (top right)

Russell Shively/Shutterstock: 82

DebbiSmirnoff/iStockphoto.com: 108 (bottom)

Stocktrek Images/Stocktrek Images/Getty Images: 153

H. Mark Weidman Photography/Alamy: 65 (top)

Wim Wiskerke/Alamy: 111

INDEX

F

G

H

S

ACKNOWLEDGMENTS

The authors would like to thank the following people for pouring their guts into this book:

Editor: Amy Cloud
Illustrator: Jack Teagle
Chief Executive Tinkerer: Meredith Halpern-Ranzer
Research and Fact-Checking: Jessica Boddy
Research: Madeline Bender and Anna Zagorski

Designers: Mary Claire Cruz and Abby Dening
Production Editors: Helen Seachrist and Erika West
Lead Production Coordinator: Melissa Cicchitelli
Copyeditor: Megan Gendell
Proofreader: Susan Bishansky
Indexer: Elizabeth Parson

A big heartfelt thanks to the folks at Houghton Mifflin Harcourt, especially Cat Onder, Emilia Rhodes, Matt Schweitzer, Lisa DiSarro, John Sellers, Tara Shanahan, Colleen Murphy, and Ed Spade.

Special thanks to our literary agent, Steven Malk.

Guy thanks his family—Hannah, Henry, and Bram.

Mindy thanks her family—Ryan, Rhett, and Birdie.